POWDER KEG

POWDER KEG

Northern Opposition
to the
Antislavery Movement

1831-1840

Lorman Ratner

BASIC BOOKS, INC., PUBLISHERS
New York/London

To the memory of my mother and father

Preface

This study of anti-abolition is limited to New England and the Middle Atlantic states during the period 1831–1840. This is not to imply that there was no anti-abolitionist sentiment in the Old Northwest (Ohio, Indiana, Illinois, and Michigan). However, because the Old Northwest was populated in part by southerners, there is in any study of that region the complicating factor of an ingrained sympathy for the slave system; the number of southerners who migrated to the Northeast, however, was negligible. Consequently, the presence of anti-abolitionist sentiment in the Northeast cannot be explained as a result of direct and sympathetic association either with slavery or with the South.

Antislavery appeals and the reaction against them were expressed before 1831 and continued after 1840; however, both the appeal and the reaction are of a special character in that decade. Abolitionists were better organized and made more concerted efforts to convince the northern public than ever before. Although the abolitionists' crusade continued after 1840, changes in the relationship between North and South caused northerners to view abolitionist proposals in a new light. Thus, though recognizing the long history of antislavery appeals and northern reactions to them, it is reasonable to consider the 1830's as a special era and to study the reaction to antislavery in that decade as a special case.

Anti-abolition was not an organized movement with prescribed principles and a definite leadership. It was a popular reaction against a set of principles and against proposed courses of action. The study of such a reaction presents methodological difficulties. The problems involved in assessing public opinion in a contemporary society are great, and the problems increase if the search is for the content of and the explanation for public opinion as it existed 125 years ago.

My objective was to discover views expressed by those who were involved with and reached some significant segment of the northern public. I examined newspapers, magazines, published sermons, and political speeches, as well as fictional and non-fictional popular writing. Private letters were not used both because public statements seemed more likely to indicate public sentiment, and because there was no reasonable way of determining whose papers should be consulted, as anti-abolition was not an organized movement. Recognizing that an individual's opinion might be shaped by his class, occupation, rural or urban surroundings, religious affiliation, or political allegiance, I selected sources reflecting the views of all such groups. The views uncovered were much the same regardless of group and so, though group affiliations are noted, the findings are of a consensus.

Having determined public opinion on a given question, there is still the problem of explaining why the public held these views. Northerners gave many reasons for their opposition to antislavery: reasons involving the Negroes' alleged inability to live in a white society, the general distrust of abolitionists because of their association with foreigners, concern for the preservation of the Union, the belief that slavery was a local not a national matter, and the general doubt that Negroes would benefit from abolition. Northerners believed their anti-abolitionist stand was logical. There were, however, other reasons, unexpressed but important in explaining anti-abolition. The last few pages of this book suggest the nature of those reasons. I am well aware of the importance of covert reasons. To attempt, however, to explore in depth that level of anti-abolition would force me to drop my primary purpose of identifying public opinion on abolition for a full-scale study of northern society in the 1830's, for anti-abolition was related to economic, political, social, and cultural conditions of that society.

Instead, I have recorded and analyzed the expressed,

overt level of anti-abolition. Studying the subject at this level, I have uncovered much about northern views of the Negro, northern sentiments with regard to reform, northern views on the role of state and national government, and northern opinion on issues such as higher versus human law.

New York   LORMAN RATNER
January 1968

Acknowledgments

I have received assistance from many persons in the years since I began this investigation as a graduate student. My greatest debts are to David Brion Davis who directed my doctoral work and whose interest in antislavery led me into that area of study. I owe much to my friend and colleague George Wylie Sypher who provided invaluable help in rethinking, reorganizing, and rewriting the original dissertation, and to my wife to whom I am indebted for her hard work and patience through a number of difficult years.

I have profited from the suggestions and criticisms of Robin Williams, Edward Fox, and Paul Gates, all of Cornell University; Douglas Maynard and Thomas B. Davis, Hunter College; W. David Lewis, the State University of New York at Buffalo; Stanley Coben, Princeton University; and David W. Becker, Miami University of Ohio.

Much of the material examined in this project was rare, and I owe an unusually large debt to the reference-library staff of Cornell University who located and obtained the many books and

Acknowledgments

microfilms I needed. I also wish to thank those librarians at the New York, New Jersey, and Pennsylvania Historical Societies, and at Harvard University, for their cooperation.

The Social Science Research Committee of Cornell University provided valuable financial assistance, as did Hunter College. Miss Audrey Schneiderman and Miss Sandra Ornstein handled typing chores efficiently and made editorial suggestions beyond the call of duty.

As anyone who has written a book knows, writing is in part a matter of endurance, and friends become almost as important as advisers. To those whose friendship I value so much, thank you.

Despite all the help and advice, I alone am responsible for any errors and shortcomings in the final product.

Contents

POWDER KEG

1

———•———

Racism Persists

In the years from the Revolution to 1820 northern states
one by one emancipated the slaves within their borders.
Vermont's constitution outlawed slavery in 1777, Pennsylvania ended it in 1780, Massachusetts in 1783, Connecticut
in 1797, New York in 1799, and New Jersey in 1804. The
founding of the New England Anti-Slavery Society in
1831 and the American Anti-Slavery Society in 1833 were

POWDER KEG

in one sense logical results of these developments.[1] The
existence of these groups establishes that some northerners
were eager to work for the total abolition of slavery in
America. Yet these organizations were better known
through their denunciation by their northern opponents
than through any widespread distribution of their literature
or their success in winning adherents. In large measure the
abolitionists' problem was that most northerners were convinced of Negro inferiority and that, whatever abolitionists
may have claimed their objective to be, northerners believed the antislavery men sought to make whites and
blacks equal. As part of his reaction to the abolitionists'
appeal Massachusetts Attorney General James T. Austin
expressed an extreme racist view that one heard often in
this decade:

> Is it supposed they [Negroes] could amalgamate? God for-
> bid. . . . But I fearlessly aver that if this be the tendency
> and the result of our moral reformation, rather than our
> white race should degenerate into a tribe of tawny-colored
> quadroons, rather than our fair and beauteous females
> should give birth to the thick-lipped, woolly-headed chil-
> dren of African fathers, rather than the Negro should be
> seated in the Halls of Congress and his sooty complexion
> glare upon us from the bench of justice, rather than he
> should mingle with us in the familiar intercourse of domes-
> tic life and taint the atmosphere of our homes and fire-
> sides—I WILL BRAVE MY SHARE OF ALL RESPONSI-
> BILITY OF KEEPING HIM IN SLAVERY.[2]

4

This racism, as vehement as any found in the South in this period, cannot be dismissed as the rantings of one isolated northern extremist. It is, in fact, the purpose of this book to demonstrate that these and related opinions were widely held in the North, and to explain how they related to and stimulated anti-abolitionism in the North of the 1830's.

It is misleading to trace a relatively rapid and steady northern progression from slavery to freedom, and from freedom to the founding of the abolitionist societies of the 1830's. In fact, the legal history of abolition in the North is deceptive unless it is borne in mind that legal emancipation alone could not, did not, and was not intended to give the Negro full citizenship. There was, and had been since the seventeenth century, a widespread and deeply planted belief in the inferiority of the Negro, whether slave or free. This chapter will examine the evidence and results of this racism, and its continuation into the 1830's. Other chapters will examine why the abolitionists of the 1830's met with opposition of an unprecedented size and virulence. Racism joined with and intensified northern fears that a national antislavery policy endangered the Union, threatened states' rights, imperiled existing political parties and churches, and would lead to catastrophic civil strife in the form of rebellions and race war. Emancipation by single northern states had not raised these problems because of the small number of their Negro population, and emancipation had not entailed federal action or foreign intervention. There had been the comforting assumption, borne out in practice, that the freed Negroes would be kept at the lowest political, social, and economic levels of society. The abolitionists of the 1830's, however, encountered opposition of unexpected intensity and extent, for their program raised broader issues and new fears.

As noted above, this opposition had its most intangible yet perhaps its strongest basis in racism. A number of historians, most recently Leon Litwack in his *North of Slavery*, have collected convincing proof of this northern racism. Nevertheless, it may be useful to review this theme briefly, in order to establish the tradition which continued into the 1830's and which was strengthened by the reaction to abolitionism.

In Massachusetts, by the end of the seventeenth century, slavery existed both in fact and in law. There, as elsewhere, whites justified slavery on the basis of the supposed natural inferiority of the Negro or Indian, or because the nonwhite was not a Christian. Northern communities excluded the unbaptized slave from their activities and found other grounds for excluding the free Negro even if he was baptized.[3]

All of the New England and Middle Colonies legally restricted the activities of free Negroes. Whites in these colonies feared that the free Negroes might serve as leaders of a slave insurrection or perhaps foment a race war. And such fears had some foundation in fact. In 1712 Negro slaves revolted in New York City, killed several whites and burned some homes. The city court sentenced several Negroes suspected of rioting to be burned to death.[4] In 1741 another slave revolt rocked New York. In its aftermath 143 free Negroes were arrested, 13 burned, 18 hanged, and 21 transported to Africa.[5]

Even before these insurrections New York and other colonies showed their concern lest Negroes and other non-whites become a menace to person and property. In 1710 New York City passed a law prohibiting Negroes, Indians and Mulattoes from being on the street at night unless carrying a lantern.[6] The law did not distinguish between free Negroes and slaves. In 1703 the Massachusetts legislature prohibited free Negroes from being on the street after nine o'clock.[7] Four years later that colony passed an act giving free Negroes restricted military duty and refusing to allow them to entertain slaves unless the master gave permission.[8] Rhode Island had similar restrictions on Negroes traveling after dark and prohibited Negroes from assembling in private homes or public places.[9]

By drafting such laws the colonists sought to lessen the danger of race violence. But this fear was not the only source of laws restricting the rights of Negroes; legal discrimination reflected widespread racial prejudice. New Jersey, which granted the Negro more legal rights than any other colony, provided in 1713 that "no Negro, Indian or Mulatto that shall thereafter be made free shall hold any real estate in his own right in fee simple or fee tail. And whereas it is found by experience that free Negroes are idle slothful people, and prove very often a charge to the place where they are . . . owners manumitting shall give security." [10]

In 1705–1706 the Pennsylvania colonial legislature marked the Negroes off as a distinct class, whether free or slave.[11] In 1725 that legislature subjected the Negro to a number of special regulations, among them a law, later adopted in many other colonies, prohibiting interracial marriage.[12] In 1717 the Connecticut lower assembly sought to prohibit Negroes from purchasing land and even living together as families without the express consent of the town.[13] These are a few examples of the manner in which northern colonies, before 1750, invoked discriminatory legislation against the Negroes.

After the Revolution northern states one by one ended slavery; but discrimination in the shape of voting prohibitions and social prejudice remained, and where discrimination had not been formalized before, it was now.

In 1780 Pennsylvania became the first state to institute gradual abolition of slavery. But despite this antislavery sentiment the transition from slave to freeman was difficult. The vote on gradual emancipation had been close; in fact, a minority protest was filed by 21 members of the state legislature.[14] In 1790 the state drafted a constitution which established the voting right of all freemen; but the state's constitution excluded the Negro from those designated as freemen and so denied him the vote.[15] In 1837 the state legislature seriously considered a bill to prevent free Negroes from entering the state and in the same session formally and directly refused the Negro the vote.[16] New Jersey, whose constitution of 1776 allowed all free males the right to vote, ruled in 1820 that suffrage should be accorded to white males only.[17] Connecticut enacted the same provision in 1814, and a high property qualification for Negro voters remained in New York's new constitution in 1821.[18]

This denial of political rights was coupled with a general restriction on the activities of free Negroes. In Massachusetts racial discrimination impelled free Negroes to establish their own Masonic order, schools, and social clubs.[19] The state outlawed marriage between Negroes and whites, and churches and ship owners adopted a policy of segregation. Negroes were even excluded from burial in the graveyards of the whites. The situation in other northern states was much the same. Whites displayed prejudice against Negroes even as they showed an awareness that slavery was an evil and that the institution ought to be abolished.[20]

This construction of barriers against the admission of the Negro into white society was the result of a long tradition of race prejudice. Thus emancipation of Negroes in the North, though it demonstrated the strong sentiment against slavery, did not reflect a willingness to accept the Negro into northern society. Racism or the conviction that racism was an insurmountable barrier to racial harmony, had characterized the thinking of many northerners for a long time.

As early as 1700 Samuel Sewall of Massachusetts wrote a pamphlet attacking slavery and the slave trade.[21] Sewall criticized the men who engaged in the slave trade or held slaves; yet even he maintained that Negroes were inferior beings for whom there was no place in white society. As the explanation for Negro inferiority Sewall cited the biblical curse of Ham. The New Englander wrote: "There is such a disparity in their conditions, colour, and hair, that they can never embody with us, grow up into orderly families, to the peopling of the land; but still remain in our body politick as a kind of extravasate blood." [22]

Even this moderate attack on slavery, tempered by its expression of belief in Negro inferiority, found opponents. John Saffin, a Boston merchant, challenged Sewall's statements regarding the slave trade and insisted there was nothing immoral about taking captives in war and making them slaves. The Negroes transported to America, Saffin said, were prisoners of war; he then proceeded to defend the slave trade on the grounds that such prisoners were better off as slaves in America than in Africa.[23]

In addition to Sewall's work, the Pennsylvania Quakers Benjamin Lay and Ralph Sandiford wrote some antislavery tracts and were consequently expelled by their meeting. Other than those few protests, antislavery activity languished before 1750.

By the latter part of the eighteenth century a growing interest in missionary work, the considerable attention given to the rights of man at the time of the American Revolution, and the increasing reform activities of the Society of Friends all served to arouse interest in the abolition of slavery and the slave trade. The slave trade was cruel, its evils were obvious, and its abolition seemed only just. Men like Jefferson, Madison, and Franklin considered slavery a contradiction of American principles. But even in an era so marked by idealism Americans wondered and worried about the prospect of a multiracial country. Racial inferiority, or practical problems involved in emancipation, or both, were grounds for hesitancy.

The first President of the new republic was one of the many Americans whose statements about slavery reflected that concern. In 1786 Washington wrote to Robert Morris concerning the attempt made by Quakers in Philadelphia to free all slaves:

> this Society is not only acting repugnant to justice so far as its conduct concerns strangers, but, in my opinion extremely impolitickly with respect to the State, the City in particular; and without being able, (but by acts of tyranny and oppression) to accomplish their own ends. . . . [*sic*]
> I hope it will not be conceived from these observations, that it is my wish to hold the unhappy people, who are the subject of this letter, in slavery. I can only say that there is not a man living who wishes more sincerely than I do, to see a plan for the abolition of it; but there is only one proper and effectual mode by which it can be accomplished, and

11

that is by legislative authority. . . . But when slaves who are contented with their present masters, are tampered with and seduced to leave them . . . it is oppression . . . and not humanity . . . because it introduces more evils than it can cure.[24]

A month later, in a letter to Lafayette, Washington wrote that "some petitions were presented to the [Virginia] assembly at its last session, for the abolition of slavery, but they could scarce obtain a reading." Washington feared that if such petitions were considered at the time, they could only lead to difficulties. He did feel, however, that eventually emancipation should be considered.[25]

In both letters and elsewhere in his correspondence Washington made clear that, though he favored emancipation, freedom for the Negro slave must come gradually and slaveholders' rights must be upheld. Washington supported the clause written into the Constitution prohibiting Congress from abolishing the slave trade until 1808. This apparently suited his belief that only by legislation could slavery safely and justly be ended.

Thomas Jefferson was more concerned with slavery and with the broader question of the Negro in America than any other political leader of the Revolutionary era. Though Jefferson thought emancipation desirable, he rejected the proposition that the Negroes, once freed, should be allowed to remain in America. In *Notes on Virginia,* written in the 1780's, Jefferson considered the question of the compatibility of the races:

The deep-rooted prejudices entertained by the whites, as well as the ten thousand recollections by the Blacks, of the injuries they have sustained . . . distinctions which nature has made; and many other circumstances will divide us into parties and produce convulsions which will probably never end but in the extermination of our race or the other.[26]

In 1789, in answer to a letter questioning him about the advisability of immediate emancipation, Jefferson noted that some Virginia Quakers had freed their slaves and put them to work as tenant farmers, but rather than work, the slaves chose to steal. Jefferson felt this was inevitable: "A man's moral sense must be unusually strong, if slavery doesn't make him a thief. He who is permitted by law to have no property of his own, can with difficulty conceive that property is founded in anything but force." [27]

Jefferson maintained that living as slaves made it impossible for the Negroes to become part of American society; but he also pointed to the inferiority of the black race as a reason for their exclusion. He gave a biological explanation for the inferiority of the Negro and went into great detail in describing how color and general physical make-up made the Negro inferior to the white. Jefferson insisted there was evidence that the Negro lacked the white's mental powers.[28] In *Notes on Virginia* he observed:

never yet could I find that a black uttered a thought above the level of plain narration; never seen even an elementary trait of painting or sculpture. In music they are generally more gifted than the whites. . . . Whether they will be

13

equal to the composition of a . . . melody . . . is yet to be proved. . . . Their love is ardent, but it kindles the sense only, not the imagination.[29]

For Jefferson, who detested slavery and felt compassion for the slave but believed the races were incompatible, colonization provided the only solution to the race problem. The colonizationists called for purchasing slaves, giving them their freedom and transporting them out of the country.

Even those who rejected the contention that Negroes were inferior recognized that the strong race prejudice of northern whites would make it impossible to bring the races together as equals. James Madison, Samuel Stanhope Smith, John Adams, and Hezekiah Niles are examples of antiracists who nevertheless came to accept the impossibility of any emancipation plan that would leave Negroes in white society.

By the 1820's James Madison agreed with Jefferson that colonization was the only way both to help the Negro and avoid racial conflict, though in his younger days he had been more optimistic than Jefferson regarding the future of the Negro in America. As late as 1790 Madison spoke out against slavery and advocated the immediate outlawing of the slave trade—a view he expounded during the Constitutional Convention. Madison was disappointed when the Convention gave the slave trade 20 years before it must cease. He told the delegates that 20 years "will produce all the mischief that can be apprehended from the liberty to import slaves. So long a term will be more dishonourable to the national character than to say nothing about it in the Constitution." [30]

The "Father of the Constitution" disagreed with Washington on this question just as the two men had disagreed years before on the question of using Negroes in the Revolutionary army. At that time Madison called for the emancipation of slaves in return for their service in the army. This would provide much-needed troops and would strengthen the colonists' ideological position.[31] In 1780 Madison wrote: "It [emancipation of slaves] would certainly be more consonant to the principles of liberty, which ought never to be lost sight of in a contest for liberty. . . ." [32] In all cases Madison stood in the minority until 1820; by then, years of observing the treatment of free Negroes in all the states caused him to take the popular stand favoring colonization. He noted the "unalterable prejudices in the U.S.," which caused him to favor the settlement of all Negroes beyond the bounds of any white settlement. Madison now concluded that the races were unable to live peacefully together since the blacks would always be dissatisfied with their inferior position and resentful of the wrongs done them as slaves. These past injustices would prevent the Negroes from becoming good citizens and would lead them to plot violence against the whites.[33] Though he rejected the argument for racial inferiority, Madison allowed his name to appear on the list of honorary officers of the recently formed American Colonization Society.

Samuel Stanhope Smith, one-time president of Princeton, was one of the few who shared Madison's early optimism regarding the prospects of an America in which Negroes and whites would live harmoniously together. In 1787 Smith published *An Essay on the Causes of the Variety of Complexion and Figure in the Human Species*. In this essay he objected to the idea, then generally accepted, that Negroes and Indians were biologically inferior to whites, and hence these races could not be granted equal status with white Americans. Smith sought to prove the common origin of all men. He accepted the physical differences between the races, but he attributed these differences to the Indians' and Negros' long residence in a primitive environment. Smith maintained that if the Indian and Negro races were exposed long enough to the white man's civilization, they would change their habits, color, and general physical appearance. Smith claimed there were records of such transformations.

In 1810 Smith brought out a second edition of this essay. In a new preface he observed that slavery prevented both the physical and social amalgamation of the Negro. Smith's associates at Princeton rejected his environmentalist theories, and there is no evidence that his views received widespread hearing or support.

John Adams, like Smith and Madison, opposed slavery

but feared the consequences of national abolition. Adams wrote in 1819 that he opposed slavery but, like so many Americans, he rejected proposals for immediate emancipation, fearing it would lead to racial violence. In a letter written in 1819 Adams made clear his position on the questions of slavery and the Negro in America:

> The turpitude, the inhumanity, the cruelty, and infamy of the African commerce in slaves have been so impressively represented to the public . . . that nothing I can say would increase the just odium in which it is and ought to be held. Every measure of prudence, therefore, ought to be assumed for the total extirpation of slavery from the United States. If, however, humanity dictates the duty of adopting the most prudent measures for accomplishing so excellent a purpose the same humanity requires, that we should not inflict severer calamities on the objects of our commiseration reducing them to despair, or to the necessity of robbery, plunder, assassination, and massacre, to preserve their lives. . . . The same humanity requires that we should not by any rash or violent measures expose the lives or property of our fellow citizens, who are so unfortunate as to be surrounded with these fellow-creatures, by hereditary descent, or by any other means without their own fault.[34]

Hezekiah Niles, editor of one of the most widely read periodicals in America, was another supporter of colonization for practical, rather than racial, reasons. In 1829, in Baltimore, Niles wrote in his paper, *Niles's Register:*

> No one can hate slavery more than I do. . . . But I can make great allowances for those who hold slaves in districts

where they abound—where in many cases, their emancipation might be an act of cruelty to them, and of most serious injury to the white population. Their difference of color is an insuperable barrier to their incorporation within the society; and mixture of free blacks with slaves is detrimental to the happiness of both.[35]

Madison, Smith, Adams, and Niles, believing whites would never accept free Negroes, reluctantly supported colonization. Men like Eliphalet Nott, president of Union College, or William Duer, president of Columbia University, saw colonization as the means of removing an inferior element from American society. Nott insisted that free Negroes "have remained already to the third and fourth, as they will to the thousandth generation—a distinct, a degraded, and a wretched race." [36] Duer considered the freedmen improvident and reckless.[37] Duer and Nott were but two of many influential northerners who, in the 1830's, commented publicly on the inferiority of the Negro and linked this belief to their rejection of abolition.

In 1835 a novel entitled *A Sojourn in the City of Amalgamation in the Year of our Lord 19—* was published anonymously in New York. *Sojourn* was written as an autobiographical piece in which the author, like Washington Irving's Rip Van Winkle, fell asleep and awoke many years later. His first observation was that blacks and whites were socializing and that amalgamation had been forced on society. As the writer saw it, the result was disastrous. The blacks became the most respectable part of the community.

Though still vulgar in dress and manners, they had attained a position of complete equality and now were in the process of subjugating the whites. Privilege after privilege was granted the Negro, and still he asked for more. White men were actually forced to marry Negro women, and fathers now came to look upon the marriage of their daughters to Negro men with great favor, though the author assured his readers that the white girls entered such unions against their wills. The scene depicted resembled a pagan orgy. Society had degenerated; people had become lazy, and the country was in a state of decline. This was the future the abolitionists were promising America: the inferior Negro destroying the superior white race.[38]

Anti-abolitionists constantly warned that racial amalgamation would result from emancipation of the slaves. Novelist and prominent politician James Kirke Paulding of New York agreed; emancipation, he insisted, would mean intermarriage. "The project of intermarrying with the blacks is a project for the debasing of the whites by a mixture of that blood, which wherever it flows, carries with it the seed of deterioration."[39] Paulding remarked that there were whites who would intermarry, but they were traitors to their race who would be universally condemned for their action. He then discussed at length the racial history of the Negro, a history that proved their inferiority. He noted that even when given educational opportunity the Negro failed to respond: "The mind of the African . . . seemed in great degree divested of this divine attribute of progressive improvement." [40] Whites were naturally superior and should not sacrifice this superiority for the sake of some abstract principle.

Concern was expressed often that abolition meant the freeing of an inferior people to mix with and degrade the white race. The editor of the influential *North American Review* was one of many northerners to issue such a warning.[41] When racial violence flared up in Philadelphia in 1838, racial mixing was cited as the immediate cause. After three days of racial violence the Philadelphia *Pennsylvanian* commented that white abolitionist women had been seen in the company of Negro men. The editor referred to the abolitionists' "socializing" with Negroes as a first step toward establishing the equality of the "African race." [42]

In March 1836 the *National Trades Union,* journal of the labor union of the same name, carried a lengthy review of James Kirke Paulding's book *Slavery.* The reviewer criticized English abolitionists who decried slavery and at the same time were willing to see children work 14 or 15 hours a day. He denounced the Irish reformer Daniel O'Connell, who supported the abolitionists, for having done nothing for English laborers but "could not bear to have his ebony brethren whipped even enough to arouse them to a sufficient degree of exertion to digest their hominy, pigs and poultry. So with our loving brethren [the abolitionists] to whom a dark skin and musky perfumes are no objections. . . ." [43]

The writer went on to accuse the abolitionists of being

wealthy men who preferred "to scatter firebrands" in their efforts to free slaves who were an inferior race, while leaving white Americans oppressed.[44] The reviewer noted that the Negro was actually better off as a slave in America than as a free man in Africa, and that the Negro slave was content in his condition. Then followed a discussion of the Negro's place in the American economy. The *National Trades Union* writer argued that certain tasks were too low for whites to perform, but that Negroes were fit and happy to perform them—shoe shining, for example. Some 15 years later George Fitzhugh, the southern apologist for slavery, made this last argument a main point in his defense of slavery.[45]

From many quarters came open expressions of strongly felt racism. An author who called himself "A Connecticut man" remarked of the Negro "That he partakes in an eminent degree of the indolence and propensity for animal indulgence . . . cannot be questioned. . . . They almost universally drink to excess, and are otherwise in gross debasement [*sic*]."[46] In the debates of the Pennsylvania State Constitutional Convention of 1837 a delegate referred to Negroes as "a race of criminals," a simple-minded people who would be used by "evil forces."[47]

In *The Last of the Mohicans* novelist James Fenimore Cooper made much of the racial characteristics of his characters—for example, Uncas, the Indian who was in love with a white girl. Cooper made it plain that marriage would have been improper between the two had not the girl a touch of Negro blood; even then the two had to die before their love could be consummated. And Cooper indicated that this trace of Negro blood had attracted the Indian to the mulatto girl.[48] Though Cooper drew the image of "the noble savage," many of the Indians in his novels showed cruelty and cunning. In his personal correspondence Cooper made clear that he considered the Indian civilization inferior to "Christian civilization," and the white race superior to any other.

Discussing Negro slavery, Cooper insisted that the great difference between American slavery and slavery in Europe (by which he meant serfdom) was that the American slave was "a variety of the human species, and was marked by physical peculiarities so different from his master, as to render future emalgamation improbable. . . . Nature has made a stamp on the American slave that is likely to prevent this consummation, and which menaces much future ill to the country." [49]

The popularity of minstrel shows added another, though indirect, comment on the belief in Negro inferiority. T. D. "Jim Crow" Rice created a stereotyped Negro comic figure for the northern stage public.[50] While playing in a theater in Cincinnati, he had seen an old Negro stablehand dancing and singing. He mimicked the Negro, adopted his name of "Jim Crow," and wrote a song "Jim Crow" based on a few words the old Negro had sung. Rice was the sensation of the northern theaters in the early 1830's. A whole series of plays about Negroes were written for him, and in

January 1833 Rice starred in a "black-face opera" called "Long Island Juba, or Love by the Bushel." [51] At the same time James Kirke Paulding's very popular play *The Lion of the West* was performed in New York. The hero, a Kentuckian called Nimrod Wildfire, made several references to how "lazy the niggers are" and the Negro servant in the play was a comic figure.[52]

For years before Rice began to appear, northern theater audiences had been used to seeing Negro clowns and black-face performers. Most circuses had a black-face clown in their troupe, and the circus performer George Washington Dixon became a stage success with his Negro act.[53] By the early 1830's many plays, even some tragedies, included a Negro song act. Northerners must have been impressed by this stereotype comic Negro, entertaining because he was so different, so inept. These caricatures revealed and must have intensified a common northern belief that the Negro was incapable of full citizenship in American society.

Racism may well have been the heart of anti-abolition, but many northerners insisted there were other grounds for rejecting antislavery. Northern critics saw in antislavery far more than just the danger of giving citizenship to racially inferior people. Abolition aroused fears for the future of the Union, the Constitution, political parties, churches—in other words, for the whole structure of American society. The next chapters will consider these various themes in anti-abolitionism.

POWDER KEG

NOTES

1. Henry W. Farnam, *Chapters in the History of Social Legislation in the United States to 1860* (Washington, D.C., 1938), pp. 218–219.
2. James T. Austin, *Remarks on Dr. Channing's Slavery by a Citizen of Massachusetts* (Boston, 1835).

    Following a mass meeting at Faneuil Hall, Boston, in December 1837 to protest the Lovejoy murder, Austin attacked the protesters and insisted that the mob that had killed Lovejoy was blameless. He compared that mob to the patriots who took part in the Boston Tea Party.
3. George W. Williams, *History of the Negro Race in America, 1619–1880* (New York, 1883), I, 121.
4. Herbert Aptheker, *Slave Insurrections in the United States, 1800–1860* (Boston, 1938), p. 14.
5. *Ibid.*, p. 15–17.
6. Williams, *op. cit.*, p. 142.
7. *Ibid.*, pp. 194–195.
8. *Ibid.*, p. 194.
9. *Rhode Island Colonial Records*, III, 492–493, quoted by Williams, *op. cit.*, p. 264.
10. Williams, *op. cit.*, p. 284.
11. Edward R. Turner, *The Negro in Pennsylvania: Slavery-Servitude-Freedom, 1639–1861* (Washington, D.C., 1911), p. 26.
12. *Ibid.*, p. 27.
13. Robert A. Warner, *New Haven Negroes, A Social History* (New Haven, 1940), p. 7.
14. Turner, *op. cit.*, p. 78.
15. *Ibid.*, pp. 174–175.

    Negroes in Pennsylvania, as elsewhere in the North, were in the lowest position on the economic scale. Their only educational opportunities were afforded them in Negro schools. Negroes were admitted into some Episcopal and Moravian churches, but not on an equal basis with whites; in most churches, they were excluded. Thus, Negroes had to form their own religious organizations. In a

24

footnote in *Democracy in America* (Vintage ed.; New York, 1957) I, 271, Alexis de Tocqueville relates a conversation with a Pennsylvanian in which the Frenchman asked why Negroes failed to vote. The reply was that Negroes had the right to vote but were afraid to exercise it. The majority of citizens were so prejudiced against Negroes that judges were unable to protect them.

16. *Ibid.,* pp. 190–192.
17. Farnam, *op. cit.,* p. 218.
18. *Ibid.,* pp. 218–219.
19. In the 1790's Massachusetts Negroes established their own Masonic lodges. For the most useful discussion of the subject see Lorenzo J. Greene, *The Negro in Colonial New England* (New York, 1942), pp. 299–302.
20. C. Vann Woodward, *The Strange Career of Jim Crow* (revised ed., New York, 1957), pp. 6–7.
   Vann Woodward argues convincingly that prejudice translated into social action has come as formal institutional governing of race relations ended. Thus, Jim Crow replaced slavery in the South after the Civil War. A similar development took place in the North in the 1820's and 1830's. A long history of prejudice made it necessary for northerners to seek to define the place of the Negro; though, as the success of the American Colonization Society in attracting northern support shows, many northerners hoped the task would be unnecessary.
21. Samuel E. Sewall, *The Selling of Joseph,* selections quoted in *Massachusetts Historical Society Collections,* 1863–1864, pp. 161–165.
22. Quoted in Charles Wesley, "Negro Inferiority in American Thought," *Journal of Negro History,* XXV (October, 1940), 542.
23. Quoted in Elizabeth Donnan, *Documents Illustrative of the Slave Trade to America* (Washington, D.C. 1931), III, 18.
24. John C. Fitzpatrick, ed., *Writings of George Washington* (Washington, D.C., 1931), XXVIII, 407–408.
25. *Ibid.,* XXVIII, 424.
26. Paul L. Ford, ed., *Works of Thomas Jefferson* (New York, 1904), III, 379–380.
27. *Ibid.,* V, 447.
28. *Ibid.,* IV, 50–60.
29. *Ibid.,* IV, 58–69.

POWDER KEG

30. Gaillard Hunt, ed., *Writings of James Madison* (New York, 1900), IV, 303.
31. *Ibid.,* I, 106–107.
32. *Ibid.,* I, 107.
33. *Ibid.,* IX, 439–441.
34. Charles F. Adams, ed., *Writings of John Adams* (Boston, 1856), X, 379–380.
35. From *Niles's Register.* Quoted in Allan Nevins, *American Press Opinion, Washington to Coolidge* (New York, 1928), p. 60.
36. Quoted in Early L. Fox, *The American Colonization Society 1817–1840* (Baltimore, 1919) pp. 32–33.
37. *Ibid.,* pp. 33–34.
38. Oliver Bolokitten [pseud.], *A Sojourn in the City of Amalgamation in the Year of Our Lord 19—* (New York, 1835), *passim.*
39. James K. Paulding, *Slavery in the United States* (New York, 1836), p. 61.
40. *Ibid.,* p. 63.
41. *North American Review* (Boston), XXXV (1832), 118–164.
42. *Pennsylvanian* (Philadelphia), May 18, 1838.
43. *National Trades Union* (New York), March 12, 1836.
   The National Trades Union had its headquarters in New York and included local unions from all over the Northeast. Ely Moore was its first president. In 1839, while a member of Congress, Moore, in a speech before the House of Representatives, accused the Whigs of trying to destroy the power of the northern workingman by freeing Negroes "to compete with the Northern white man in the labor market." Quoted by Arthur Schlesinger, Jr., *The Age of Jackson,* p. 425.
   Microfilm of all issues of the Union's newspaper are available at the library of The New York School of Industrial and Labor Relations, Cornell University.
44. *National Trades Union,* March 12, 1836.
45. George Fitzhugh, *Cannibals All! Or Slaves Without Masters!* (Richmond, Virginia, 1857.)
46. [Anon.], *An Inquiry into the Condition and Prospects of the African Race in the United States and the Means of Bettering Its Fortunes* (Philadelphia, 1839), pp. 14, 24.
47. *United States Gazette* (Philadelphia), June 21, 1837.

26

48. James Grossman, *James Fenimore Cooper* (New York, 1949), pp. 44–46.
49. James Fenimore Cooper, *The American Democrat* (new ed.; New York, 1931), p. 166.
50. George C. Odell, *Annals of the New York Stage* (New York, 1928), III, 628–632.
51. *Loc. cit.*
52. James K. Paulding, *The Lion of the West* (new ed., Stanford, Calif., 1954), p. 37.
53. Carl Wittke, *Tambo and Bones* (Durham, N. C., 1930), p. 19.

2

———·———

Meddling Outsiders

Despite their prejudice toward the Negroes, northerners accepted the end of slavery in their own states on a local, state-by-state basis. But the abolitionism of the 1830's called for men of one state to impose their will upon men of other states and, at least in the eyes of the northern public, for men of one country to interfere with the affairs of another.

The English antislavery movement achieved a major victory when, in 1833 Parliament set forth steps to end slavery in the Empire. The English abolitionists played an important role in helping to organize the American antislavery groups. English tracts were distributed by American abolitionists. English and other European writers criticized America for permitting slavery and, on occasion, English abolitionists spoke from American platforms. The American abolitionists were closely associated with English antislavery men. As the New England antislavery leader Samuel May asserted, George Thompson and other English abolitionists crossed the ocean to show Americans their transgressions.[1]

In the 1830's, however, American abolitionists found this association with the English antislavery movement a costly one. The decade was characterized by an extreme sensitivity to foreign criticism and supposed foreign conspiracy. In an age when Americans, troubled by political and economic problems, feared for the future of their institutions and were overly quick to defend them, such an association could only arouse public ire.

In the 1830's European observers wrote articles and books decrying the state of American society.[2] Such critics as Harriet Martineau, Frances Trollope, Thomas Brothers, Basil Hall, and Gustave de Beaumont singled out slavery as a notable fault and criticized Americans for permitting it to continue. Americans were highly sensitive to such attacks; they answered their critics with counterarguments and even with outbursts of mob violence against foreigners or those connected with them. Both northerners and southerners associated American abolitionists with foreigners and denounced the antislavery men as un-American. The abolitionists, who welcomed help from their English counterparts, were attacked verbally, and at times with physical violence, as foreign conspirators or dupes of those conspirators.

In articles, novels, and travel accounts European critics made plain their dislike of slavery and their low regard for Americans who condoned it. The works of these European writers circulated in the North and were often attacked by northern writers.[3] Foreigners frequently wrote unfavorable accounts of their visits to this country, which made Americans even more hostile to foreign censure of slavery. Americans were already belligerent toward foreign observers who often pointed out the high incidence of violence in the United States, decried the lack of culture, the maltreatment of the Indians, and the corruption in American politics. A few samples from the vast foreign travel literature will demonstrate the kind of criticism Americans received with regard to slavery and the way they reacted to it.

In her *Domestic Manners of the Americans,* Frances Trollope made clear her distaste for American manners and institutions. Her commentary on the crudeness of American men, the gaudiness and general bad taste displayed by the women, and the lack of culture presented a grim picture of the Republic. In America, she remarked, "that polish which removes the coarser and the rougher parts of our nature is unknown and undreamed of." [4] Though she rather enjoyed the gracious plantation life of the South, Mrs. Trollope condemned the institution of slavery, especially what she termed "its licentious aspects." [5] Americans were acquainted with *Domestic Manners,* and both James Kirke Paulding, in *The Lion and the West,* and Asa Greene, in his satirical novel *Travels in America,* ridiculed Mrs. Trollope. [6] Paulding created Mrs. Wollope, a stuffy Englishwoman who criticized everything American. Though she said she disliked slavery, she treated her servants worse than slaves, and slaves she met worse than their masters would treat them. Paulding contrasted Mrs. Wollope's hypocrisy with the candor of his frontier hero, Nimrod Wildfire. [7] Greene dedicated his work to Mrs. Trollope, sarcastically assuring her that to place his name on the same page with hers was sure to give him immortality. [8]

Another English traveler, Harriet Martineau, wrote much more flattering accounts of America than Mrs. Trollope. In *Society in America* Mrs. Martineau praised many aspects of American life, but she, too, criticized our tolerance of slavery. [9] From 1835 to 1837 the abolitionists prevailed upon her to write a series of articles supporting their crusade. These articles were collected and published in 1838 as *The Martyr Age.* In these articles Mrs. Martineau wrote of her dislike of slavery and stated that England had imposed the institution on America, and that it was a carry-over of corrupt institutions Americans were in

31

the process of eliminating. It was a measure of American sensitivity that this moderate position did not prevent Mrs. Martineau from being denounced as violently and often as were George Thompson, Daniel O'Connell, and other foreign critics. The northern press attacked her for praising William Lloyd Garrison and for supporting the antislavery movement in general, and referred to her as a meddling foreigner and a threat to the Republic.[10]

During the eighteenth century French writers had been the most prominent apologists for America. But in time the French, especially those of the "romantic school," came to look upon America as a society that had lost its golden chance.[11] Pastoral, virtuous America of the natural man without the fetters of institutions to bind him had been lost, and French critics now pictured America as a dull, money-conscious, middle-class society, similar to the France of the July Monarchy.[12] Americans, instead of communing with nature, had transformed their country into the counterpart of the well-mowed lawns of the eighteenth-century landscape.[13]

When those two most famous French travelers to America, Gustave de Beaumont and Alexis de Tocqueville, returned home, they each set about to record their experiences and make public their observations. While Tocqueville sought to analyze all aspects of American life, Beaumont wrote *Marie, or Slavery in the United States.* Here he expressed his disillusionment with America which had resulted from his observations of the treatment of the Negro.[14] Beaumont stressed that white Americans believed the Negroes were inferior. Marie, the heroine of his story, had a drop of Negro blood. She married a white, and because of this miscegenation, husband and wife both suffered and eventually were killed. In the course of the narrative Beaumont wrote of the many Americans who, though opposed to slavery, were so prejudiced that they would consider emancipation only if the Negroes were transported to Africa. He maintained that these antislavery, yet prejudiced, people felt slavery was a stain on the nation's honor. But, Beaumont noted, they resented any foreigner pointing this out, and he believed that their opposition to slavery was motivated by self-interest. "They are ridding themselves of an annoyance, an embarrassment . . . they have worked for themselves, not for the slaves." [15] Beaumont made clear to his French readers that the southern slaveholder was an unromantic figure who served as an example of feudal corruption, lacking both gallantry and honor.[16]

Beaumont joined with the English writers in condemning America as a society of hypocrites who preached democracy while they sanctioned slavery. Naturally, Americans resented these attacks, and defenders of the country, like Asa Greene or the influential New Yorker Calvin Colton, answered the charges.

In 1833 Calvin Colton, while a newspaper correspondent in London, published *The Americans*.[17] In this book he developed a line of defense that was reiterated time and again in the northern press and magazines of the 1830's.

Colton began by assuring his English readers that, despite the frequent reference to the Revolution in Fourth-of-July oratory, Americans actually felt no animosity toward the British.[18] He also denied that Americans were overly sensitive to foreign criticism. After refuting Mrs. Trollope's and Captain Hall's fallacies in regard to American manners, he discussed American institutions. Colton, a supporter of the American Colonization Society, which sought to free slaves and send them and all free Negroes to Africa, chided the British for being so critical of America when it was they who had introduced slavery into the Colonies. Though he confessed that the republic had done less than it should have to promote emancipation, he noted that many states had in fact outlawed slavery. Circumstances in the United States, he said, made emancipation less simple than it had been in England, but the American Colonization Society, was making real progress toward that goal. Colton pointed out that criticism of slavery in America was actually being used by English politicians for their own ends. The English radicals cited American institutions in their fight for reform, and more conservative English politicians countered by pointing out the weaknesses and failures of those institutions. In this way, Colton denied that there was any substance in the British criticism and insisted that Americans were handling the slavery problem adequately.[19] Returning to the subject of slavery in a long appendix, Colton defended colonization, accepted the basic inferiority of the

Negro, and warned that in all good projects there are always some mischief-makers, i.e., the abolitionists.[20]

Sometimes specific European writers on slavery were the target, but usually northern writers simply denounced foreign interference in general. John Quincy Adams, though he aided the abolitionists, noted in his diary in 1835:

> It [the abolitionist movement] has linked itself with religious doctrines and religious fervor. Anti-slavery associations are formed in this country and in England, and they are already cooperating. . . . They have raised funds to support and circulate inflammatory newspapers and gratuitously . . . send multitudes of them into the Southern country, into the midst of swarms of slaves. . . .[21]

Catherine Beecher, daughter of the prominent clergyman and reformer Lyman Beecher, wrote that the general disposition of the people in America was to believe the English were interfering in American affairs through the abolitionist societies.[22] The *Boston Transcript* denounced all foreign criticism of American slavery and proposed that foreigners should be refused the right to speak on the subject.[23] Miss Beecher and the editor of the *North American Review* both noted that the English had introduced slavery into America and so had no right to be critical.[24] William Lloyd Garrison's presence in New York, on his return from England in 1833, helped to touch off a riot in that city. One New York paper implied that Garrison had gone to England to learn how to undermine the institutions of his own country.

Some northerners went beyond simply rejecting foreigners as legitimate critics of America. By the 1830's stories of an English abolitionist conspiracy circulated in the North —indicating indeed how highly sensitive Americans were in the 1830's to criticism of their institutions. By 1835 some newspapers were carrying stories claiming that abolitionists were part of a foreign plot. Since these stories circulated in a number of northern newspapers, the idea of a foreign plot in which abolitionists were involved seems to have struck a responsive chord in northern society. In the 1830's Americans were generally prone to the belief that, in any case, they were beset by all sorts of foreign threats and plots.

In 1834 the painter, writer, and inventor, Samuel F. B. Morse began publishing a series of letters in the *New York Commercial Advertiser,* writing under the pseudonym "Brutus." These letters described a foreign conspiracy, master-minded by Prince Metternich in collusion with the papacy and aimed at the overthrow of republican government in America. By 1844 all 12 letters, collected in book form and entitled *Foreign Conspiracy Against the Liberties of the United States,* had gone through six editions.[26]

The fact that Morse had traveled in Europe seemed to give his story added validity. Also, many writers before him had conditioned Americans to accept the idea of conspiracies at work, especially foreign conspiracies. For centuries

European Protestants had feared a Catholic plot to destroy Protestantism, and after the Bavarian Illuminati scare of the 1790's Americans were particularly concerned about the existence of such plots.[27] The signs of anti-Catholic feeling in the 1830's are well-known.[28] Many believed the Catholics were conspiring to destroy both Protestantism and democracy. These same Americans were susceptible to anti-Masonic and anti-Mormon appeals.[29]

Since northerners often spoke of foreign powers seeking to destroy the republic, opponents of antislavery found this appeal to the fear of conspiracy an excellent way to arouse public sentiment against the abolitionists. Furthermore it was an effective means by which to silence the antislavery advocates, for conspirators were considered unworthy of the right even to be heard.

James Watson Webb, editor of the *New York Commercial Advertiser,* and James Gordon Bennett, of the *New York Herald,* were leading proponents of the idea of an abolitionist conspiracy. Both editors told similar stories of abolitionist plotting, though Bennett's was the more sensational. In October 1835 Bennett claimed knowledge of an English plot to flood America with tracts and money to fight for abolition, the ultimate purpose being the destruction of the Union.[30] This, he insisted, was the beginning of a great conspiracy. Ten days later, he claimed to have exposed a plot by a secret group who planned to use this money to purchase the *New York Evening Post* and turn it into an abolitionist propaganda organ. From time to time during the next few years, *Herald* editorials were devoted to reviving the fear of this conspiracy. Then in the fall of 1838 as part of a campaign against the Locofocos, an insurgent group in the state's Democratic Party, Bennett claimed that the abolitionists, Locofocos, and English radicals were allies in a plot to destroy America. In one issue Bennett warned:

> This is no fancied picture. We are on the brink of danger. . . . The abolitionists of England are operating here. *We know the fact.* Between now and the election we shall develop a conspiracy that will astonish the whole Union.[31]

Soon after Bennett sailed for England, letters appeared in the *Herald* providing evidence of a great international abolitionist conspiracy. Abolitionists were even accused of fomenting a revolution in Canada against English rule.[32]

Obviously, Bennett hoped to sell newspapers to anti-English readers, and this reporting of an abolitionist plot was the publicity stunt of one single editor. However, such writers as Catherine Beecher, in her *Essay on Slavery,* the editors of the *Boston Transcript,* the *Eastern Argus* of Portland, Maine, and the magazine *North American Review* also put forward the idea of an English abolitionist conspiracy. James Kirke Paulding, who had been so critical of Mrs. Trollope, pointed to an English abolitionist conspiracy in his book *Letters from the South.* Paulding launched into an attack on the British for their interference. He insisted that this was part of a plot of European despots against Americans and their institutions, a plot launched because these despots were in danger of being overthrown: "This hostile feeling toward our national character and institutions had lately assumed a new and more mischievous disguise. It came masked under the semblance of humanity toward the slave." [33]

George Thompson's reception upon his visit to America was perhaps the most convincing evidence of how strongly northerners resented foreign criticism of slavery and foreign activity in the American antislavery movement. When a mob in Boston attacked William Lloyd Garrison in October 1835, the police probably saved his life by shouting, "He's an American, he's an American." Actually, the mob had wanted not Garrison, but the English reformer and abolitionist George Thompson. Thompson, who had been touring the New England states on behalf of the abolitionists, had already faced hostile crowds in New Hampshire and Massachusetts.[34] Almost every newspaper in New England condemned him, and his announced visit to Boston led to warnings that he would meet a crowd ready to use violent means to silence him, were he to attempt to speak there.[35]

In their attacks on Thompson northern newspaper and magazine editors constantly emphasized his nationality. Insisting that an Englishman had no right to interfere in America's internal affairs, they reminded their readers that foreigners like Thompson had called Americans sinners or apologists for sin, and that Englishmen failed to appreciate the complicated nature of the American slavery problem. The editors usually concluded by attributing Thompson's calls for immediate abolition to his ignorance or his desire to see American institutions destroyed. The Philadelphia *United States Gazette* condemned the Boston riot, but called Thompson an interfering foreigner and later reiterated a charge printed in the *New York Commercial Advertiser* that Thompson had urged slaves to cut their masters' throats.[36] Both papers insisted that Thompson had once stolen money. Lynde Walter, editor of the *Boston Transcript,* accused Thompson of being "a wandering insurrectionist" and pointed specifically to what the editor believed to be an attempt to break up Andover Theological Seminary.[37] Soon thereafter, the *Transcript* published the following notice:

THOMPSON THE ABOLITIONIST

That infamous foreign scoundrel Thompson will hold forth this afternoon at *The Liberator* office no. 46 Washington Street. The present is a fair opportunity for the friends of the Union to smoke Thompson out! It will be a contest of the Union. A purse of $100 has been raised by a number of patriotic citizens to reward the individual who shall first lay violent hands on Thompson so that he may be brought to the tar kettle before dark! Friends of the Union be vigilant! [38]

Editor Walter insisted no American should put up with such action by a foreigner. This was four months before the Boston riot. During these four months Thompson began

40

his tour and riot-inciting anti-Thompson remarks were published by many newspapers, including the Providence *Rhode Island Country Journal,* the *New Bedford Mercury,* the *Boston Transcript,* the *New York Commercial Advertiser,* and others.[39] The editor of the *Eastern Argus* referred to Thompson as a man touring through the "Northern and Middle States at the expense of the good old ladies of Glasgow." [40]

The New Hampshire legislature singled Thompson out in its report on abolition, called him a foreign conspirator, and those American abolitionists who invited him to this country "deceivers of the American people." [41] Thus, the Boston riot was the outgrowth of the frequent intolerant remarks made by respectable sources. This antiforeign reaction obviously reflected a strong American nationalism.

The 1830's are frequently characterized as a period of buoyant optimism based on the great economic and geographic expansion of the time. During this decade, also, many Americans believed that their political institutions might serve as a model to the rest of the world, that this was America's mission. All this optimism and these beliefs were expressed in the form of a vigorous nationalistic spirit. Yet, the defense of those American institutions sometimes took the shape of an antiforeign, anti-abolitionist crusade. The South was, of course, part of America, a region to which northerners looked with pride, and criticism of the South could be construed as an attack on America. Abolitionists who denounced the South, whether foreign or

American touched a sensitive spot; for northern respect and admiration, even pride in that region, were surprisingly great. Northerners in the 1830's thought the object of abolitionist efforts—the Negro—inferior, and the object of abolitionist attacks—the southern planter—superior.

In *Cavalier and Yankee* William Taylor has argued that the northern public, for the most part, was favorably inclined toward the planter. Taylor's findings and my own observations come together to suggest that the North in the 1830's had a romantic image of the South.[42] Northern novelists often glorified the South. It was not the South alone that created the image of the gentleman planter: he was a national myth with a national connotation. To many northerners the planter, by living close to nature and at the same time displaying all the social graces, proved that the freedom of the American frontier was compatible with order and morality: American freedom would not lead to French revolutionary license. The northerner read of planters who, though wealthy, shunned excessive display or pursuit of wealth, but instead selflessly turned to law and politics. In other words, the northerner found the southern planter the ideal citizen of a republic of virtue. Therefore, many northerners refused even to listen to abolitionist denunciations of the slaveholder.

The romance of southern plantation life was given full play in James Kirke Paulding's *Letter from the South,* and in John Pendleton Kennedy's *Swallow Barn* which was one of the most popular novels of the day. Kennedy, a native of the Delaware Valley, described a plantation life that had lost some of its greatness, but that still had much of the old romantic tradition about it. John A. McClung described the idyllic plantation life in his novel *Camden, A Tale of the South,* and the anonymous author of *Rose-Hill* offered a similar picture of southern life. These were only a few of the many novels glorifying the South.

Novelists were not the only northerners sympathetic to the South. A New Hampshire legislative committee concluded by assuring southerners that northerners "are not yet prepared to hear with complacency the intelligent planters, the able politicians, the high-minded men of the South, denounced as traitors to the cause of religion, as harsh and unfeeling masters." [43]

Even though most northerners disliked slavery, they were extremely careful to point out the dangers of ending the institution and to insist that it was a southern matter. This position was developed into an argument as to the constitutionality of ending slavery and the legal and social ramifications of its abolition. We will consider these arguments in the next chapter. Whatever the reasons, many northerners insisted that any attempt by abolitionists outside the South to end slavery constituted meddling by outsiders.

In April 1833 the *New York Evening Post* printed an editorial concerning relations between North and South. The paper noted that "certain nullification journals . . . are trying to excite the prejudice of the South against the

North in relation to the question of slavery." [44] In addition, the editorial continued, a small group in the North was advocating immediate emancipation and opposition to the Colonization Society. This latter group, the editors assured the South, had been trying for several years to win widespread support in the North, but without success. The paper decried the efforts of a few extremists to create North-South tension.

But the slavery question remained after the nullification controversy had ended, and the *Post* made frequent reference to the problem. In June 1833 the paper came out editorially for colonization. In August, *Post* editor William Cullen Bryant attacked the abolitionists. Noting that most Northerners regretted the existence of slavery in America, the editor insisted:

> There is not the slightest disposition to interfere in any improper and offensive manner, except among certain fanatical persons, and those few in number, we regard it to be as well settled as any fact in relation to public opinion ever discussed in the public journals.[45]

A contributor to the New York *Knickerbocker Magazine* warned his readers with regard to abolitionists, "Each man has his hobby, in riding which, it would be well for him not to trample on the rights of his neighbor." [46] The *Eastern Argus* of Portland, Maine, denounced the abolitionists even more vigorously. The *Argus's* editor noted the agreement among almost all northern papers in their anti-abolitionist stand and called slavery a southern problem. However, he decried anti-abolitionist meetings, insisting that the South wanted a silencing of any discussion of slavery, whether favorable or unfavorable.[47]

Many northerners insisted that the slavery problem must be left to southerners to solve. In 1832 the Colonization Society journal the *African Repository* referring to the new abolitionists for the first time, expressed its strong disapproval of "the crude and fantastic notions of a few *radicals* or *ultras* . . . who undertake not only to judge what the South must do, but to do it for them." [48] A writer who called himself "a Connecticut man" and a former abolitionist proclaimed that any northern interference would only slow down emanciption and that southerners were best equipped to handle the problem.[49] The *Boston Transcript* and the *Knickerbocker Magazine* also made this point.[50] James Fenimore Cooper insisted, in a chapter on slavery in his book *The American Democrat,* that for the North slavery was only an abstract question of principle while for the South it was of the highest practical importance. Thus it was the South that was best prepared to deal with slavery, and northern interference in this delicate matter could lead only to the worst kind of disorder.[51]

Cooper accused the abolitionists of prejudice by which he meant the tendency of one group to try to force its ideas on another. In discussing this question the author took the reformers to task. What right, he asked, had one part of the country to try to force its customs upon another? [52]

As to the right to petition, Cooper noted that Congress was "not bound to waste its time in listening to and in discussing the matter of petitions, on the merits of which that body has already decided," while states were legally prevented from petitioning. "The danger of the practice is derived from the tendency of creating local feelings, through the agency of local government, and of thus endangering the peace of the union." [53] Once again it was a matter of imposing on the rest of the country the standards of one section, standards that might be set up by a small but vocal minority within that section.

Catherine Beecher warned in her attack on the abolitionists that the North should not interfere in the affairs of the South. Moral suasion, the method used by all reformers, would be effective only when an individual exhorted the community of which he was part; an outsider would only cause resentment. Thus, the abolitionists had no business exhorting the South and indeed were only causing resentment there.[54]

The arguments put forward by northerners against outside interference in a southern problem was in some quarters carried far beyond just insistence on the southerner's right to handle his own affairs. Abolition seemed to endanger all of American society, for its demands to end slavery raised legal questions, fears of a future Negro-white society, and other seemingly dangerous issues of national concern.

NOTES

1. Samuel May, *Recollections of the Anti-Slavery Conflict* (Cambridge, Mass. 1869), p. 144.
2. Though not all visiting foreign writers despaired at conditions in America, there were enough denunciatory statements to arouse the public. Almost every American newspaper and magazine of the period I have examined (more than 50) attacked one or more hostile foreign critics.
3. The editors of several magazines attacked all Englishmen who denounced Americans for condoning slavery. See the *North American Review* (Boston), XLI (1835), 170–171; *American Quarterly Observer* (Boston), January, 1833, pp. 95–101. See *Atkinson's Saturday Evening Post* (Philadelphia), June 13, 1835, p. 141, for a bitter attack on Gustave de Beaumont and his antislavery novel *Marie*.
4. Frances Trollope, *Domestic Manners of the Americans* (4th ed., London and New York, 1832), p. 56.
5. *Ibid.,* pp. 29–30.
6. Asa Greene, *Travels in America* (New York, 1833). The *New York Mirror,* October 19, 1833, p. 127, praised Greene's book.
7. James K. Paulding, *The Lion of the West* (new ed.; Stanford, Calif., 1954), *passim*.
8. Greene, *op. cit.,* p. 1.
9. Harriet Martineau, *Society in America* (New York, 1837), *passim*.
10. Such attacks appeared in the *North American Review,* XLI (July, 1835), 181; the *Boston Transcript,* February 5, 9, 1839; the *New York Herald,* October 20, 1838; the *New York Review and Quarterly Church Journal,* III, 5, 130–133.
11. Seymour Drescher, "America and French Romanticism during the July Monarchy," *American Quarterly,* XI (Spring 1959), 3–21.
12. Drescher cites Balzac, Chateaubriand, Dumas père, Hugo, Lamartine, and others.
13. *Ibid.,* p. 18.
14. Gustave de Beaumont, *Marie, or Slavery in the United States* (new ed.; Stanford, Calif., 1959), *passim*.

15. *Ibid.*, p. 78.
16. *Ibid.*, pp. 123–124.
17. Calvin Colton, *The Americans* (London, 1833). Colton, a prominent New Yorker and member of the American Colonization Society, denounced the abolitionists in two books: *Colonization and Abolition Contrasted* (Philadelphia, 1835), *passim,* and *Abolition a Sedition* (Philadelphia, 1839), *passim.*
18. Colton, *The Americans,* p. 14.
19. *Ibid.*, p. 156. This argument was frequently used by northerners in their attacks on the British.
20. *Ibid.*, pp. 156–157. Of some 50 newspapers examined, only one, the *New York Herald,* was opposed to the work of the Colonization Society. In their attacks on the abolitionists these papers often mentioned that the work of the antislavery men might endanger the possible success of the colonizing scheme. Thus, Colton was stating a familiar argument.
21. John Quincy Adams, *Diary* (Allan Nevins, ed., New York, 1951), p. 462.
22. Catherine E. Beecher, *An Essay on Slavery and Abolitionism* (Philadelphia, 1837), p. 145.
23. *Boston Transcript,* March 11, 1836.
24. C. Beecher, *op. cit.,* pp. 44–45; *North American Review,* XLI, 1835, 170–171.
25. The *New York Commercial Advertiser,* quoted by the *Liberator* (Boston), October, 1833.
26. Samuel F. B. Morse, *Foreign-Conspiracy against the Liberties of the United States* (6th ed., New York, 1844).
27. See Vernon Stauffer, *New England and the Bavarian Illuminati* (New York, 1918), for the best discussion of the efforts of Jedidiah Morse and other New England Federalists to raise the specter of a Masonic conspiracy.
28. The standard work is Ray Allen Billington, *The Protestant Crusade 1800–1860* (New York, 1938).
29. See David Brion Davis, "Some Themes of Counter-Subversion: An Analysis of Anti-Masonic, Anti-Catholic, and Anti-Mormon Literature," *Mississippi Valley Historical Review* XLVII (September 1960), 205–224, and Lorman Ratner, "Anti-Masonry in New York,

An Aspect of Pre-Civil-War Reform" (unpublished master's essay, Cornell University, 1958), for discussions of the conspiracy theme in the anti-Masonic movement of the 1820's.

30. *New York Herald,* October 17, 19, 1835.

31. *Ibid.,* October 19, 1835.

32. *Ibid.,* October 20, 1838.

33. James K. Paulding, *Slavery in the United States* (New York, 1836), pp. 117–118.

34. See Theodore Lyman, Jr., *Papers Relating to the Garrison Mob* (Cambridge, Mass., 1870), p. 21.

35. Thompson spoke in Concord and Nashua, New Hampshire, Lowell and Lynn, Massachusetts, and many smaller towns on his tour of the northern New England states.

36. *United States Gazette* (Philadelphia), February 5, 1836.

37. *Boston Transcript,* July 21, 1835. On August 8 the *Transcript* reported that a mob had broken up a Thompson meeting in Lynn; in late August a meeting of prominent Bostonians at Faneuil Hall produced a resolution calling for the silencing of Thompson. In October, when rumors circulated that Thompson was in Boston, a notice was posted calling for all citizens to join in tarring him and running him out of town. Then came the Garrison riot, precipitated because the opponents of antislavery believed Thompson would be the main speaker at an abolitionist meeting.

38. See Lyman, *op. cit.,* p. 14.

39. On March 11, 1836, the *Transcript* denounced Thompson, the Irish leader Daniel O'Connell, and the English radical Fanny Wright, for being meddling foreigners, because they spoke in America against slavery. The *New Bedford Mercury* (Mass.), October 30, 1835, denounced Thompson as an English fanatic. The *Newburyport Daily Herald* (Mass.), October 24, 1835, followed the same line; so did the *Eastern Argus* (Portland, Me.), August 7, 1835, and many other New England and New York papers I examined.

40. *Eastern Argus,* August 7, 1835.

41. Samuel May Collection Tract #261 (Cornell University Library, Ithaca, N. Y.).

42. See William R. Taylor, *Cavalier and Yankee* (New York, 1961). Taylor argues convincingly that northerners had a great deal to do

POWDER KEG

with the creation of the myth of the South and the southern planter. My studies of the literature of the period led me to a similar conclusion before reading Taylor's work.

An interesting discussion related to Taylor's thesis is raised by Perry Miller in "The Romantic Dilemma in American Nationalism and the Concept of Nature," *Harvard Theological Review,* XLVI (October, 1955), 239–254. Miller discusses Americans' fear that romantic nature is gone, and with it those virtues ascribed to nature and so distinctly American. The ideal image of the republic was of a virtuous, often agrarian, people. This virtue would be lost if we became a commercial nation. The similarity of Miller's views with those of Taylor, and most recently Charles Sanford, in *The Quest for Moral Paradise* (Urbana, Ill., 1961), is obvious.

43. Samuel May Collection Tract #261.
44. *New York Evening Post,* April 25, 1833.
45. *Ibid.,* August 7, 1833.
46. *Knickerbocker Magazine,* XI (1837), 321.
47. *Eastern Argus,* August 7, 1835.
48. *African Repository* (Washington, D.C.), VIII, 143.
49. Anon., *An Inquiry into the Condition and Prospects of the African Race in the United States and the Means of Bettering its Fortunes.* (Philadelphia, 1839), p. 149.
50. *Boston Transcript,* December 22, 1832; *Knickerbocker Magazine,* XI (1838), 328.
51. James F. Cooper, *The American Democrat* (new ed.; New York, 1931), p. 170.
52. *Ibid.,* p. 53.
53. *Loc. cit.*
54. C. Beecher, *op. cit.,* pp. 12–14, 35–36.

3

———•———

The Union, States' Rights, and Individual Rights

The first two chapters have concentrated on anti-abolitionism's foundation on racism, its resentment of foreigners
interfering in America and of outsiders meddling in southern affairs. This chapter will consider another series of
responses to antislavery: the argument that abolition endangered the Union, challenged states' rights, and intruded
on the rights of individuals. The abolitionists saw their

51

cause as the freeing of enslaved Negroes, but in working to free the Negroes they unintentionally raised meaningful and complex legal and constitutional problems. The abolitionists could have been rationally challenged on these points; yet, here as elsewhere, anti-abolitionism was usually expressed in slogans and emotional appeals rather than in rational argument. James Kirke Paulding's attitude was typical:

> It [abolition] has become the fruitful theme of calumny, declamation and contention; the stalking horse of political parties and fanatical reformers. It has . . . disturbed the peace of communities and states. It menaces the disruption of our social system, and tends directly to a separation of the Union. . . . The obligations of the truth have been sacrificed to unmitigated reproach, and the laws and Constitution of the country attempted to be trampled underfoot, in the hot pursuit of the rights of humanity. The feeling and good name of millions of our fellow-citizens have been grossly assailed, their rights invaded, their firesides and social institutions disturbed, and their lives endangered without any regard to the dictates of our moral code. . . . In asserting the natural rights of one class of men, the Constitutional rights of another have been denounced as violations of the law of God . . . unbrotherly warfare has been, still is waging against a large portion of the good citizens of the United States, which, if continued, must inevitably separate this prosperous and happy union.[1]

The 1830's have been characterized both as a time when Unionism, personified by Andrew Jackson, grew strong and when states' rights, personified in John Calhoun and the nullification controversy, was also on the upswing. These two ideas were compatible, and indeed both were strongly evident at the same time. The Union was viewed in a mystical sense. It was the compact of states engaged in the task of economic growth and territorial expansion. States' rights, however, was a legalistic concept. The old Jeffersonian localism called for government to operate primarily on the local level. The Union would accomplish the great goals of society while the states would be responsible for its day-to-day operations. Many northerners feared that the abolitionists threatened the existence of the Union by raising an issue that might force a group of states to secede. The abolitionists seemed to threaten the localist equality position by demanding federal action on slavery, which was almost universally viewed as a state matter.

Whatever the actual danger of disunion in the nullification controversy, it raised the specter of disunion just as the new abolitionists appeared. Although the antislavery men made no appeal at this time to expel the South from the Union (on the contrary, the sinners were to be saved), the northern public thought that antislavery efforts would further agitate an already aroused South.

Following a lengthy discussion of nullification, the editor of the *Boston Transcript* warned:

> It cannot be doubted that if the course provided by the editor of *The Liberator,* and his collaborator was generally countenanced by the people of the non-slaveholding states . . . it would tend to the speedy disintegration of the

Union. New England would be disloyal to the federal compact. . . . The fact is that comparatively speaking, few persons sanctioned these measures, who understand their actual bearing on the slaves, the free blacks, or the white citizens of the South.[2]

Two years later, when George Thompson was due to appear in Boston, the *Transcript* carried the text of an anti-Thompson circular mentioned earlier in which the writers made clear that to attack Thompson was to defend the Union.

Northern politicians, partly reflecting their constituents' views and partly fearful of party division should slavery become an issue, objected to abolition as dangerous to the Union. Thus Edward Everett, while serving as governor of Massachusetts in 1837, made a special point of attacking the abolitionists. Everett insisted the Union could have been founded only with the compromise on slavery, and that abolition would divide the Union.[3] State Attorney General James Austin also warned of civil war if abolition prevailed.[4]

Massachusetts Democrats agreed with their political opponents on many of these points. Democratic leader Robert Rantoul, Jr., claimed the abolitionists were looking for an opportunity to destroy the Union.[5] As early as 1831 George Bancroft made it clear that, though unsympathetic to slavery, he was unwilling to attack it. In 1834, Bancroft delivered his only speech on the subject before 1854. The historian-politician noted that slavery had destroyed Rome, but he was careful neither to ask nor to imply that Americans should end the institution at once. Bancroft's most recent biographer, Russel Nye, claims that Bancroft thought a moderate stand on antislavery might win some votes, but instead Bancroft discovered that it cost him support; he then avoided the subject until the 1850's, when popular sentiment had changed.[6] Bancroft was one of a number of prominent Americans whose attitude toward antislavery changed from hostile to friendly.

Martin Van Buren frequently remarked on his dislike of the abolitionists, and his political allies constantly pointed out that he was a Union man strongly opposed to any movement that might encourage secession.[7] The Democratic president of the Pennsylvania State Senate, James Burden, remarked that the Union could never have been formed if the Founding Fathers had not compromised on the slavery question. "Modern abolitionism," Burden insisted, "had upset the spirit of compromise." [8]

Calvin Colton went even further and insisted the abolitionists were conspiring to destroy the Union, and that destruction of the Union was their avowed goal. In a book entitled *Abolition a Sedition* Colton announced that he would prove that abolition was "at war with the genius and letter of the Federal Constitution and of the Constitutions of the States respectively, and with that compact which created the Union." [9] He believed that by proving this "then clearly there will be presented a constitutional basis on which the movement can be opposed, and by which, if

it shall become necessary it can be suppressed." [10] Colton
began his discussion by stating that the antislavery movement had started as a religious crusade, but those who
sought to use it for political ends had perverted it: "These
men turned abolition into a political organization independent of any government, usurping the powers of government." He concluded that the Anti-Slavery Society had
become an independent power—self-erected, self-governed,
independent, and irresponsible—which sought to destroy
the union.[11] He quoted from a number of abolitionist letters and tracts to prove that from its origin the Society had
intended political action.[12]

The alleged abolitionist threat to the Union was often
coupled with the accusation that the antislavery men were
calling upon the federal government to infringe on the
rights of states. The anti-abolitionists were not necessarily
contradicting themselves by supporting the Union while
maintaining the right of states to determine slavery policy.
As ardent a Unionist as Daniel Webster insisted that slavery was a state matter and that only the states involved
could legislate to end the institution within their borders.[13]
Webster was willing to defend the abolitionists' right to
petition Congress as long as those petitions called for ending slavery in the District of Columbia, the only area in
which he thought Congress had such authority. On several
occasions Webster called for the end of slavery in the federal district, but he wrote off any other abolitionist plans as

illegal.[14] Typically, Webster opposed the abolitionists as well as slavery.

James Fenimore Cooper insisted that slavery was a state matter outside federal government jurisdiction, though he did think that Congress, by constitutional amendment, could put an end to slavery. But, he continued,

> It would be madness for Congress, in the state of the Country, to attempt to propose an amendment of the Constitution, to abolish slavery altogether, as . . . it would infallibly fail, thereby raising an irritating question without an object.[15]

In 1835 Governor William L. Marcy of New York received requests from several southern governors to return alleged fugitive slaves. Marcy agreed to return the slaves and called on the state legislature to approve his decision. In his message the governor called the abolitionists fanatics and defended southern states' rights.[16] The New York *National Trades Union* denied that Congress even had the right to end slavery in the District of Columbia.[17] The New Hampshire state legislature, as part of a lengthy denunciation of abolition, assured the South that they considered slavery purely a state matter.[18] Paulding's fear that abolition could be accomplished only at the price of disunion and the violation of states' rights was thus taken up and echoed by other critics of antislavery.

The abolitionists were vulnerable to attack as a menace

to the Union and to the rights of states; in addition, abolition's apparent threat to the rights of individuals was frequently cited. One of the abolitionists' basic arguments was
that the slave was a human and that his slave condition
deprived him of his rights, the rights of an American. Anti-
abolitionists found a number of grounds on which to chal-
lenge this contention. As we saw in Chapter One, northern
racists denied that the Negro was an equal of the white.
Some northerners argued that the inferior Negro should be
deprived of equal status, that he needed to be kept enslaved
for his own good, and that to offer him equal rights would
endanger the right of northern workingmen to jobs, or
deny southern slaveholders their right to a healthy economy or to security from race violence.

James Fenimore Cooper took the stand that the abolitionist insistence on the right of the Negro to equal status,
or even to freedom, raised a theoretical problem about the
meaning of equality. To Cooper equality was a relative
thing; all men were obviously not created equal; the blacks
and whites, for example, were unequal. In America, under
the democratic system, there was more equality than in
other countries, but Americans quite properly rejected
absolute equality. "The very existence of government at all,
inferred inequality." [19]

Slavery, Cooper noted, was an institution as old as
human history and would probably continue just as long as
some men were in a more advanced state of civilization
than others. Slavery was no more sinful "than it is sinful to

wear a whole coat, while another is in tatters, to eat a better meal than a neighbor, or otherwise to enjoy feast and plenty, while our fellow creatures are suffering and in want." [20] This, then, was the kind of inequality that Cooper believed democracy should leave as is. "According to the doctrines of Christ, we are to do as we would be done by, but this law is not applied to slavery more than to any other interest in life. It is quite possible to be an excellent Christian and slaveholder, and the relations of master and slave, may be a means of exhibiting some of the mildest graces of the character." [21] Cooper could see how, in some ways, the slave benefited from his condition, and he cited the argument that the Negro was better off a slave in civilized America than a free man in barbarous Africa.[22]

Like almost all those who wrote on slavery, James Kirke Paulding discussed the question of whether it was a contradiction of the doctrine of equal rights. He argued that equal rights meant that those who could get rights were entitled to them and denied automatic equality of rights for all. In war slaves were taken, and this was not looked on as a violation of equal rights.[23]

Calvin Colton also engaged in the discussion about equality. As for the argument that slavery was a contradiction of American doctrines, Colton made the point that liberty meant not freedom, but willingness to submit to a government of laws. Laws in themselves were a kind of subjection. Equality meant not some romantic notion of natural rights, but simply the destruction of any kind of

59

feudal privilege; that is, the denial of legal privileges to any special group.[24]

Cooper, Paulding, and Colton met the abolitionist claim that Negroes deserved equal rights by challenging the abolitionist interpretation of equality. From many other quarters came arguments that Negroes either were inferior, and so did not deserve equality, or that because of their inferiority legal equality would actually harm the Negro. One writer in the *North American Review* insisted that "abolitionist proposals would lead Negroes to believe they were equal to whites with dire consequences for both." [25] The editor of the *American Quarterly Observer* argued that slavery was best for the Negro; that the Bible did not condemn the institution; that slave owners were neither unjust nor cruel; that other republics had had slavery; that white society profited by having slaves to do menial tasks, for thus white labor could do more respectable and useful work, and this prevented extreme class differences among whites.[26]

Though few northerners defended slavery this vigorously, Lynde Walter of the *Boston Transcript* did insist that the Negro was unfit for citizenship.[27] James Austin noted that abolition would not end the whites' belief in the Negroes' inferiority.[28] Novelist Robert Montgomery Bird, in a section of his book *Sheppard Lee,* insisted slaves wanted to remain in that condition and considered freedom a punishment.[29] In January 1834 the editor of the American Colonization Society's journal the *African Repository* declared, "Let the abolitionist give up his cause as impossible of execution, hateful to the community, ruinous to the cause of the blacks, and founded upon principles wrong in themselves." [30]

It was even argued that, accepting the need to free the slave, the abolitionist movement would delay rather than further that end. Calvin Colton, among others, insisted that the abolitionists had made discussion of slavery with southerners impossible, had forced the South to take a more radical stand on the issue, and so had actually hurt the cause of the Negro.[31] Another New Yorker, Doctor David M. Reese, a prominent physician and an active temperance advocate, said that he favored the kind of antislavery opinion expressed by such national heroes as Franklin, Jefferson, and John Jay.[32] These men, though they worked for ending slavery, tolerated the slaveholder. They recognized that slavery was an evil but felt that holding a slave was not a sin in itself. Reese insisted that these great men were the true abolitionists and true philanthropists.[33]

Robert M. Bird thought that the abolitionists were selfishly motivated. In *Peter Pilgrim,* Bird chided the abolitionists, saying:

I was somewhat of an abolitionist myself, quite desirous to see all the poor blackies as free as blackbirds; but then I saw clear enough, they never could be liberated, without ruining their masters, as well as all the agricultural interests of the South, unless some means could be devised for supplying their loss, by finding substitutes for them.[34]

61

The substitute was a mechanical "nigger" who would do all the work and prevent all the moral problems. Bird's central character presented his scheme to the abolition society:

> They could not bear that they should lose the honour, and glory, and profit of completing the great work of emancipation that I, who was not actually a professed member of their society or that anybody save themselves, should reap the splendid regard; and, accordingly, they knocked my model to pieces, maltreated myself, and ended by charging me with madness and bringing me to this place in a strait jacket.[35]

The debate as to the true meaning of equality, that the Negro slave should not have equality, or that abolition was not the best way to attain this, all were indeed theoretical arguments. But at least one group of northerners, the spokesmen for the northern workingmen, viewed the question as a practical one.[36] To this group abolition posed two basic problems. First, it deflected attention away from the plight of northern white laborers who, these men insisted, needed more help than the slaves. Second, if abolitionists succeeded in freeing slaves, the freedmen would flood the northern labor market and deprive northern whites of their right to earn a living. Some workingmen's groups were among the most outspoken and vitriolic of all anti-abolitionists.

The leaders of the crusade for the preservation of America as the land of the simple yeoman artisans made it clear that they spoke of white yeoman-artisans. To include the Negro would be to raise a divisive issue that the working-men's movement wished to avoid.

The *New York Post*'s acting editor William Leggett insisted that, rather than working for the Negro, the abolitionists were actually "aristocrats," and that antislavery was an aristocratic plot to overthrow the Democrats. In February 1835 Leggett branded the abolitionists as tools of those business interests whose only concern was a supply of cheap labor.[37] George H. Evans, Seth Luther, and the editor of the *National Trades Union* all pictured abolitionists as men who sought to use the spirit of philanthropy for their own selfish purposes. Luther and the *National Trades Union* editor stressed that antislavery was a diversion from the true object of reform.

In 1833, in his *Address to the Workingmen of New England on the State of Education,* Luther decried the lowly condition of the northern laborer as even lower than European labor or slave labor in the South. In the same year he wrote: "We have the philanthopists moaning over the fate of the Southern slave when there are *thousands* of children in this State as truly slaves as the blacks in the South."[38] Evans, the editor of *The Workingman's Advocate,* published in New York, told his readers that abolitionists were men "actuated by a species of theological fanaticism, [who] hoped to free the slaves *more* for the purpose of adding them to their religious sect, than for love of liberty and justice."[39]

Other labor reformers joined the attack on the abolitionists. Orestes Brownson, in the October 1838 issue of
the *Boston Quarterly Review,* pointed out that the wage
system in the North was far worse than chattel slavery.[40]
Labor-paper editor A. H. Wood noted that although workers should oppose slavery, they must also face the fact of
job competition from free Negroes.[41] In the issue of September 17, 1836, the editor of the *National Laborer* stated
that he opposed slavery, yet he urged the white laborer to
look after his own condition before worrying about that of
the Negro slaves.[42] In 1838 William Leggett wrote to
abolitionist leader James Birney that he was powerless to
stop the editor of the *New Era,* a labor journal, from attacking the abolitionists.[43]

Though not involved in the workingman's movement,
James Paulding claimed that the slave was not completely
at the mercy of the master, that there were certain legal
restrictions on the master, and that the slave was better off
than the northern or English industrial worker.[44]

Since northerners believed abolitionists threatened and
might even destroy the legal, constitutional basis of the
country, it was logical for those who opposed antislavery to
assume that abolition would bring about the destruction of
law and the Constitution, and thus general disorder would
sweep the land. Northerners often equated abolitionists
with violence—even though it was the reformers who were
the targets of the violence—and gave the violence cited as
a reason why abolitionist appeals must be rejected.

NOTES

1. James K. Paulding, *Slavery in the United States* (New York, 1836), pp. 5–6.
2. *Boston Transcript,* December 22, 1832.
3. Paul R. Frothingham, *Edward Everett* (Boston and New York, 1925), p. 131.
4. James T. Austin, *Remarks on Dr. Channing's Slavery by a Citizen of Massachusetts* (Boston, 1835), pp. 45–46.
5. Luther Hamilton, ed., *Memoirs, Speeches and Writings of Robert Rantoul Jr.* (Boston, 1854), p. 719.
6. Russel B. Nye, *George Bancroft* (New York, 1944), pp. 104–106.
7. *Albany Argus,* July 23, 1835.
8. J. R. Burden, *Remarks of Dr. J. R. Burden of Philadelphia County in the Senate of Pennsylvania on the Abolition Question, February 18, 1838* (Philadelphia, 1838), p. 6.
9. Calvin Colton, *Abolition a Sedition* (Philadelphia, 1839), p. 2.
10. *Ibid.,* p. 2.
11. *Ibid.,* p. 3.
12. *Ibid.,* p. 6.
13. Claude M. Fuess, "Daniel Webster and the Abolitionists," *Massachusetts Historical Society Proceedings,* LXIV (1930–1932), 28.
14. J. W. McIntyre, ed., *The Writings and Speeches of Daniel Webster* (Boston, 1903), XII, 210.
15. James F. Cooper, *The American Democrat* (New York, 1931), p. 188.
16. Quoted in the *Albany Argus,* December 29, 1835.
17. *National Trades Union,* July 12, 1834.
18. Samuel May Collection Tract #261 (Cornell University Library).
19. Cooper, *op. cit.,* p. 42.
20. *Ibid.,* p. 162.
21. *Ibid.,* pp. 165–166.
22. *Ibid.,* p. 166.
23. Paulding, *op. cit.,* p. 25.
24. Colton, *op. cit.,* p. 122.

25. *North American Review* (Boston), XXXV (1832), 128–142.
26. *American Quarterly Observer* (Boston), I (1833), 95–101.
27. *Boston Transcript,* December 22, 1832.
28. Austin, *op. cit.,* p. 44.
29. Robert M. Bird, *Sheppard Lee* (New York, 1836), I, 23.
30. *African Repository* (Washington, D.C.), IX, 330.
31. Colton, *op. cit.,* p. 122.
32. David Reese, *The Humbugs of New York* (New York, 1838), pp. 143–164. Reese stressed the differences between such abolitionists as Jefferson, Franklin, Jay and those "modern abolitionists," whom he termed "ultra." The ultra abolitionists, he warned, were flooding the country with literature, trying to move into the churches, and were supported by "pseudo-philanthropists."
33. *Ibid.,* pp. 163–164.
34. Robert M. Bird, *Peter Pilgrim* (2 vols., Philadelphia, 1838), I, 106.
35. *Ibid.,* p. 107.
36. Walter Hugins, *Jacksonian Democracy and the Workingman's Party,* New York, 1960, and William Sullivan, "Did Labor Support Andrew Jackson?" *Political Science Quarterly* (New York), LXII (December, 1947), 569–580, note the non-labor character of these parties. Edward Pessen, however, in "The Workingman's Movement of the Jacksonian Era," *Mississippi Valley Historical Review,* XLIII (December, 1956), insists the parties were truly composed of workingmen. In either case, the reform character of those parties seems clear. Whether purely a political body or a labor movement, the workingmen's parties were supporters of a great variety of reforms and dreamed of the good society.

    For more detailed accounts of the relation of labor to slavery see Bernard Mandel, *Labor, Free and Slave* (New York, 1955); William H. Lofton, "Abolition and Labor," *Journal of Negro History,* XXXIII (July, 1948), 249–283, and Joseph Rayback, "The American Workingman and the Anti-Slavery Crusade," *Journal of Economic History,* III (November, 1943), 152–163. All three stress the diversity of attitudes among labor reformers on the abolition question. All agree that labor leaders were generally opposed to abolition.
37. *New York Evening Post,* February 10, 1835.
38. Seth Luther, *Address to the Workingmen of New England on the*

State of Education, quoted by Arthur Schlesinger, Jr., *The Age of Jackson* (Boston, 1953), p. 425.

39. *Workingman's Advocate,* New York, November 21, 1835.
40. *Boston Quarterly Review,* October, 1838.
41. See Bernard Mandel, *Labor, op. cit.,* pp. 81–84.
42. See Philip Foner, *History of the Labor Movement in the United States* (New York, 1947), p. 273.
43. See Dwight Dumond, ed., *The Letters of James Gillespie Birney* (Washington, D. C., 1938), I, 477.
44. Paulding, *op. cit.,* p. 123.

4

———•———

Fears of Radicalism and Violence

The abolitionists continually faced the traditional northern belief in the inferiority of the Negro, and their efforts intensified rather than weakened it. Those who subscribed to this dogma of the Negro's inferiority frequently objected to abolitionism, claiming it was impractical in a biological sense, as well as politically and morally. Accordingly, abolitionists were described as impractical, as madmen, pseudo-philanthropists, and in other such terms.

The *Norwich Courier,* in Connecticut, defended the right of abolitionists to be heard but referred to their cause as "an insane project—one which no man in full possession and exercise of his faculties can contemplate as being practicable, or at the present desirable." [1] The *Connecticut Observer* and the *Hartford Observer* concurred in referring to abolition as "madness." [2] The *New England Magazine* in Boston, referred to the antislavery advocates as "rhymers, antiquarians, saints militant, and the like." [3] The editor considered these men "insane philanthropists espousing highly dangerous fanatic doctrines." [4] *American Quarterly Observer*, also published in Boston, used similar language and arguments when discussing antislavery.[5] The editor of the *Emporium and True American,* in Trenton, New Jersey, referred to abolitionists as "rum-mad fanatics who have become so infatuated that they will stop at nothing short of the emancipation of the whole slave population." [6]

Logically, since the anti-abolitionists argued that their opponents were impractical and visionary, they might have concluded that abolitionists could well be left to themselves without harmful results. But, as we have seen, there was a real fear of civil disunion and even armed conflict in the North of the 1830's. In addition to their deep apprehension about the Constitution, now increased by South Carolina's nullification efforts, northerners felt an even deeper terror of slave insurrection and race war in all parts of the country. Nat Turner's insurrection in 1832, and the revolt in the British West Indies, provided a plausible foundation for this fear. In 1835, in Baltimore, Maryland, Hezekiah Niles wrote in *Niles's Register*:

> During the last and present week we have cut out . . . more than *five hundred* articles, relating to the various *excitements* now acting on the people of the United States. . . . *Society seems everywhere unhinged.* . . ! We have the slave question in many different forms, including the proceedings of *kidnappers* and *manstealers* and others belonging to the *free Negroes* . . . an awful political outcry is about to be raised to rally the poor against the rich. . . . The character of our country seems suddenly changed, and thousands interpret the law in their own way. . . . The Republic seems threatened.[7]

Accordingly, anti-abolitionists frequently seem to have felt that their opponents, although too unrealistic to achieve their goal, were dangerous in the context of the times. Thus they feared abolitionists, in their efforts to free the slaves, might "succeed" in nullifying the federal Union, dislocating northern society, and instigating rebellion and race war in the South.

The intensity of these fears was both a cause and a symptom of the fact that abolitionists were loosely identified with all sorts of radicals and social undesirables. Whig politicians equated the abolitionists with Locofocos, a supposedly radical insurgent group of New York Democrats, Democrats with Federalists. Conservatives believed that the abolitionists were Jacobins, while radicals saw them as agents of a conservative plot to overthrow democracy. James Gordon Bennett, though he too opposed abolition, chided his countrymen for their hysteria that led them to fear Catholics, abolitionists, bankers, gamblers, "or the what-nots." [8] Gordon was correct about the inaccuracy of these accusations; yet, they were effective in focusing sentiment against the abolitionists. They account for and symptomize the fact that the abolitionists were often dissociated from other, more widely-accepted, contemporary reforms, and that they were so consistently charged with endangering the political structure of the Union and the social fabric of America.

The case against the abolitionists was covered extensively by the editor of the *New York Commercial Advertiser*:

> Notwithstanding the strong censure applied by the whole country to the numerous publications from the same mischief-working press . . . the same coterie of pseudo-philanthropists have here put forth a more formidable and still more offensive publication in the face of warnings of North and South. . . . Not content with having distracted the churches, destroyed the peace of families and communities, embarrassed the literary and religious institutions, menaced the property and even the existence of the union, involved the officers of our government in dangerous perils, and created the most appalling apprehensions of a civil and servile war, they are still unmoved. . . .[9]

The writer noted that he had once considered the abolitionists well-meaning but misguided, but their latest publication, coming at this time of *crisis,* proved the antislavery men were determined to resist public opinion and risk the future of the country to attain their ends.[10] The *New York Evening Post* accused abolitionists of using fanatical tactics and the *New York Commercial Advertiser* denounced Garrison as a newspaper man unfit to set type.[11] Connecting Garrison with Nat Turner's revolt in Virginia, a slave uprising in which 57 whites and over 100 Negroes were killed, the editor insisted that "Garrison's rockets, harmless in the North, are torpedoes and infernal engines at the South and patriotism requires that they should be destroyed before they explode."[12]

Governor William L. Marcy of New York, in a statement in 1835, assured southerners that northerners considered abolitionists fanatics:

Our citizens are generally aware of the mischief these proceedings [Anti-Slavery Convention] are doing among our southern brethren. Large and highly respectable public meetings in all parts of the State have already been assembled and have expressed their sentiments on the subject in the fullest possible terms of reprobation. . . . The feeling of almost the entire population here, is what the South could wish it to be. The powerful energy of public opinion has been brought to bear directly on this subject and has exerted and is now exerting a benign influence in repressing the fanaticism that has arisen in this section of the Union.[13]

Marcy referred to the abolitionists as "sinister, reckless, agitators."[14]

The editor of the *North American Review* in Boston observed that the Colonization Society, in contrast to abolition, "send abroad no influence to disturb the peace, or endanger the security or prosperity of any portion of the country." [15] A reviewer of *Slavery,* a book by the abolitionist Lydia Maria Child, criticized Mrs. Child for adhering to antislavery doctrines and listed his objections to abolition. He claimed abolitionists sought to arouse "public passions." [16]

James Kirke Paulding's anti-abolitionist attacks culminated in his insistence that abolition, like the other "violent reforms" with which it had associated, as a result of its perfectionist doctrines would lead to anarchy, dissension in society and in the churches, and even to destruction of the family. In the final chapter, "On the Fanaticism of the Abolitionists, and Its Hostility to Religion, Morals, Liberty, Patriotism, and Social Virtues," Paulding accused the abolitionists of inciting violence, of undermining the New and Old Testaments, of violating the sanctity of the home, and of defiling the country.[17]

The president of the Pennsylvania State Senate, James Burden, offered the most sweeping condemnation of all. As part of a long denunciation of abolition he stated:

> It has held out expectations to the colored people which cannot be realized—it has led their young men to a course which has produced reaction—it has given to the wanton and unthinking excuse for persecution— . . . it has been humane in the abstract, but dreadfully cruel in the reality.[18]

73

If abolitionists were to continue, Burden warned the State Senate, southerners would be driven to such a state of fear that they would force all free Negroes to migrate to the North. This, he pointed out, in a year of severe economic depression might lead to additional wage competition which would further degrade both the free Negroes and the many whites then out of work. The white female would be forced to face "the dreadful choice of prostitution or starvation. Vice will increase greatly. Working men will be discouraged, families will shrink in size." [19] In other words, Burden described the breakdown of the entire social order, the destruction of everything from the family to the Union—all as a result of abolitionist activities.

Pennsylvania was not the only state in which political leaders branded abolitionists as reckless and fanatic agents of disunion, perpetrators of race war, and agents of a foreign power. Both political parties denied any association with the antislavery men and sought to brand their opponents as abolitionists. Unless these many political leaders completely misread the signs of the time, the northern public must have been generally and strongly anti-abolitionist.

Of all these alleged results of abolitionist radicalism, the most feared was actual violence. As we have seen, northerners in the 1830's had a fear of civil war, made more concrete now by South Carolina's nullification efforts, and strong fears of slave insurrections and race war. As we saw in Chapter Three, over the years there had been a number of incidents of unrest. These incidents together with the

Nat Turner rebellion of 1832 were placed by some at the abolitionists' door and seemed to justify apprehension.

Although abolitionists insisted that emancipation could be accomplished without violence, northern critics sometimes noted that violence had followed emancipation in the British West Indies. The New York *National Trades Union* claimed that emancipation in the West Indies had resulted in race violence and that a full-scale revolution was feared.[20] James Kirke Paulding took special note of the situation in the West Indies; he believed that emancipation there had done great harm to both Negroes and planters and had caused violence and general disorder.[21] Following the Nat Turner rebellion, the *New York Evening Post* carried a lengthy editorial which pointed out that there had been enough slave unrest to "cause the people of the more northern states to be ready, in case of need, to extend to the [southern whites] ample assistance in men and munitions."[22] Though the paper made no mention of abolitionists for a time, it carried reports that whites led the revolt. The Augusta, Maine, *Kennebec Weekly Journal* insisted that "we should give our southern brethren some assurance that while we depreciate the existence of slavery among them . . . we set our faces against all measures calculated to occasion the calamities they apprehended."[23] Another editor associated the American abolitionists with the radical movement responsible for the French Revolution, the demand for greater liberty in England, as well as with the agitation to emancipate American slaves.[24]

In August 1835 the *Boston Transcript* warned that immediate abolition would lead Negroes to insurrection and that the white population of the South was in danger. Though unsympathetic to the South, the *Transcript* wanted to make clear that southerners misjudged the North if they thought that section in any way condoned abolitionist doctrines which the South blamed for inciting servile insurrection, specifically the Nat Turner revolt.[25] The *Transcript* expressed concern over the "brute passions" of Negro slaves. The editor of the Maine *Eastern Argus* accused the abolitionists of fomenting slave revolts and remarked that the attempt of a Boston slave to kill his owner was the "fruit of abolition." [26]

For the *New Jersey Journal* the abolitionists were the cause rather than the victims of violence. The paper predicted servile war and even civil war, should abolition sweep the North.[27] The *Newburyport Daily Herald*, commenting on the anti-abolition riots in New York in October 1833, stated that, though opposed to mob violence, it had "no sympathy with the anti-slavery party." [28] The editor reminded his readers he had always disapproved of abolition schemes. He now warned those schemes would lead both to civil and servile war. The *Daily Herald* reported that the people of Boston "without distinction of parties, are decidedly opposed to the unreasonable designs of the immediate abolitionists." [29] Later in the year, after the Garrison riot, the paper, like many others, objected to the use of force, but referred to Garrison and George

Thompson as "infuriated fanatics." [30] The *Herald* carried similar remarks regarding mob action and abolitionists in issues following the murder of Elijah Lovejoy, an abolitionist newspaper editor killed in Alton, Illinois, in 1837 while defending his press and the burning in 1838 of Pennsylvania Hall built by Philadelphia abolitionists as a place in which they could meet.

In a report of January 1837, a committee of the New Hampshire House of Representatives stated: first, since slavery had existed for a long time, the present generation of southerners should not be held responsible for it; second, it would take a long time before slavery would disappear; third, slaves might easily be aroused by abolitionist efforts and resort to violence which would mean the death of many whites and the destruction of much property.[32] The New Hampshire *Portsmouth Weekly Journal* added its warning that abolition would mean slave insurrection.[33]

This horrifying accusation that slave uprisings would result from abolitionist agitation explains why so many northerners opposed abolition so strongly; yet, there was the even more appalling charge that abolition might lead to general race war. During the summer of 1835 the *Pennsylvanian,* one of the two leading Democratic papers in Philadelphia, noted the excitement then being stirred up concerning abolition. The editor called the abolitionists madmen and accused them of fomenting a servile war in the South. The paper warned that if the antislavery men continued their efforts the southern states, for their own safety, would have to exile all their free Negroes who would then come north. These free Negroes, the editor wrote, would "thus increase a population among us which already has been the cause of repeated tumults and disorders." [34] The *Pennsylvanian* urged its readers to oppose abolition and support colonization.

In 1832 the *North American Review* published a reply to a letter praising the American Colonization Society. The *Review*'s writer, after providing a history of the Society, insisted that most slaveholders wanted free Negroes removed from the country in order to avert race war. Pointing out that the colored man was biologically inferior to the white, the author called on the public and the government to combine and help return these Negroes to Africa. [35]

James Gordon Bennett wrote in his *New York Herald* that the abolitionists "stirred the Negroes up so that they are seeking white mates." [36] The theme of sexual relations between the races made good copy, and Bennett mentioned it often thereafter. In the spring of 1838 the *Herald*'s editor claimed abolitionists were bringing Negroes into the city and arming them in preparation for a race war. [37] The New York *Knickerbocker Magazine,* noting the danger of racial violence, called the abolitionists "amateur philanthropists" and likened them to "an experimental philosopher . . . who was anxious to wager . . . that he could perforate a keg of gun powder . . . without endangering the contents or the lives of the lookers-on." [38] Like most northerners, the *Knickerbocker*'s editor considered the price of abolition more than the product was worth. The editor of the *National Trades Union* also worried about race conflict and referred to the "mad and tantalizing course of the immediate abolitionists." [39]

Warnings of race war were not limited to newspaper editors, who might have exaggerated to attract readers. President Noah Porter of Yale published a letter in which he warned that abolition would lead to race violence.[40] James Fenimore Cooper insisted that despite the relative mildness of American slavery, if the day arrived when slavery was ended and the two races had to live together, there would be a race war resulting in the extermination of either whites or Negroes. Cooper warned that Negro inferiority would make it impossible to ever amalgamate the Negro and consequently he was bound to clash with the white.[41] James Austin of Massachusetts made the same point, as did the staunch anti-abolitionists James Kirke Paulding, Calvin Colton, and Robert Montgomery Bird. All feared what one writer referred to as "the peculiar relation of the black and white races in this country."

Anti-abolitionists saw the antislavery men as the perpetrators of doctrines that would produce anarchy. But, ironically, the most obvious and immediate acts of violence were those committed by anti-abolitionists. Violence was resorted to in order to prevent violence. As Doctor David M. Reese of New York put it, "pseudo-philanthropists" backed the current abolitionist movement. The leaders of this new movement were intemperate when discussing slavery and, as a result, their fanaticism led to more fanaticism.[42] Anti-abolitionists found themselves in the difficult position of either defending the abolitionists' rights or committing mob violence. They often tried to escape the dilemma by rejecting mob violence, but blaming such action on the abolitionists.

After 1835 the abolitionists devoted much of their effort to circulating and then presenting petitions to various legislative bodies. Increasingly, the question of abolition became one of whether these white Americans should be heard. Thus the slavery issue was partially obscured by the struggle for the maintenance of the civil rights of whites. Northern mobs were willing to use violence to silence antislavery men like Garrison and Thompson; but no responsible citizen could condone such actions. The press and the politicians disliked what the abolitionists said but were reluctant to infringe upon their right of free speech. The attempts to solve this dilemma ranged from John Quincy Adams' resolute defense of that right, through evasions of the question, to an insistence that the antislavery men brought violence upon themselves.

In 1835 John Quincy Adams confided to a friend, "With the slave and abolition whirligig I hope to have no concern but upon other questions I cannot be silent and must speak my mind." [43] Adams made it clear that he supported abolition out of a sense of duty to governmental process rather than out of sympathy with antislavery. In addition, the New Englander expressed concern that his

defense of principle might cost him re-election since many
of his constituents objected to aiding antislavery men for
any reason. Like Adams, Caleb Cushing, the only other
New England congressman willing to present abolitionist
petitions, helped the abolitionists because he believed they
had a legal right to be heard, though he disagreed with
what they said. Cushing also believed he jeopardized his
political future by going against popular sentiment in his
state regarding abolition.[44]

Concern for the rights of abolitionists did temper some
anti-abolitionist attacks. When the Democrats led the fight
to silence Adams in 1837, the *Boston Atlas* criticized the ex-
President, but at the same time accused his critics and Democratic political opponents of denying a basic right. The
paper accused Democrat James Buchanan of Pennsylvania
of betraying the North when he attacked the right of petition.[45] Lynde Walter of the *Boston Transcript* often mentioned that, though he disagreed with abolitionists, he
would defend their civil rights. But to carry this out was
another matter. The *Transcript* supported Adams in the petition controversy, but later rejected abolitionist claims that
the government's halting of abolitionist materials sent
through the mails was also a violation of guaranteed rights.
In addition, the editor insisted that abolitionists should be
prevented from sending their literature through the South.[46]

Free speech was the ultimate concern of men like
Adams. But many other northerners, when faced with the
problem of abolitionist rights were ambivalent; some in-

fringed on the Constitution which they were so eager to
protect, and others embraced the very tactics they deplored
when abolitionists used them. Accordingly, the position of
the members of the Massachusetts state legislature was
more typical than Adams' stand. When the abolitionists
tried to submit petitions to that body, the legislaure imposed their own "gag rule" and denied the abolitionists the
right of petition.[47] Long-time Massachusetts Federalist
leader Harrison Gray Otis, reflecting the legislature's sentiments, demanded an end to antislavery agitation in any
form and from any source.[48]

The *Boston Transcript* denounced mob violence but at
the same time blamed Garrison and Thompson for inciting to riot. As to freedom of speech, editor Lynde Walter
called Thompson a "quack" who had no right to speak.
Walter said nothing about Garrison's rights nor did he
comment on Lovejoy's rights, but mob violence was difficult to disregard. In November 1837 when Elijah Lovejoy
was killed the *Transcript* reprinted a description of the
event but offered no editorial comment. When Pennsylvania Hall was burned in 1838, Walter devoted his editorial
page to decrying what he believed was the cause of the
violence: the mixing of the races. It seems the mob rioted
because of reports that white women and Negro men were
walking together.[49] Thus Walter saw the Philadelphia in-
cident as a result of abolitionist defiance of accepted customs in race relations. But incidents such as this made the
anti-abolitionists uncomfortable.

82

The *Boston Atlas* also discussed the burning of Pennsylvania Hall. The *Atlas* decried the act, exonerated the abolitionists from blame, and attributed the whole affair to the work of radical Democrats.[50] Shortly before the 1840 election, the paper claimed that the whole abolitionist agitation was part of a plot of "southern aristocrats" and northern radicals to destroy the Union.[51] It seems that the *Atlas* preferred developing this plot to discussing antislavery directly.

Perhaps no northern newspaper editor was more aware of the dilemma posed by violent attacks on abolitionists than the intensely anti-abolitionist James Gordon Bennett, founder and editor of the *New York Herald*. Bennett was as fanatical as anyone in his attacks on abolitionists and yet, despite his claims that the abolitionists were involved with foreign conspirators and that antislavery men were stirring up race war, he refused to condone violence used against them. Shortly after the Lovejoy murder, the *Herald* accused the "Wall Street Press" of having stirred up the public.[52] However, here and elsewhere Bennett made clear his concern that such attacks strengthened the abolitionist position. Before 1837 Bennett had shown considerable uncertainty as to how to handle this problem. Facing the anti-abolitionist riots in October 1835, the *Herald* called on the public to silence the abolitionists by means other than force.[53] In 1836 Bennett warned his readers that the riots had failed to end abolition and that, in fact, the anti-slavery advocates were stronger and more radical than ever.[54]

Clearly, after 1837 Bennett was convinced that violence against abolition was strengthening rather than weakening the movement. His objections to violence were primarily tactical, not constitutional.

The *New York Evening Post* also opposed antislavery, though this paper was more moderate in its anti-abolition than the *Herald*. Through the violence-filled summer of 1835 acting editor William Leggett pressed his attack against antislavery but called for calm, legal action to silence the movement.[55] In 1837, after the Lovejoy killing, the *Post* warned that violence was morally wrong and strengthened the abolitionist cause, making legal suppression of it more difficult.[56] The paper called on the northern press to encourage calm reason rather than mob action, both for moral reasons and as a practical measure to stop the spread of abolition. Like Bennett, the *Post*'s editors Leggett and William Cullen Bryant had changed their attitude on the question of violence. Bryant had commented, after an anti-abolitionist riot in New York in 1833, that mob action was to be expected when men as radical as the abolitionists insisted on making public speeches.[57]

The right to express an unpopular view was fundamental in a free society but many northerners believed that, if it were expressed, society would be destroyed. Some northerners were convinced that abolitionists not only provoked violence but that their doctrines, if carried out, would produce it. Thus newspaper editors, politicians, and others found themselves caught between their defense of legal process and their fear that abolitionists would destroy that process. As the historian Russel Nye has shown, eventually mob action against abolitionists forced many anti-abolitionist northerners to be sympathetic to, if not actually in agreement with, the antislavery position.[58] But in the 1830's the abolitionists still seemed the primary menace to social order.

NOTES

1. *Norwich Courier,* July 31, 1833.
2. *Connecticut Observer,* quoted by the *Norwich Courier,* July 16, 1834; *Hartford Observer,* quoted by the *Courier,* July 30, 1834.
3. *New England Magazine* (Boston), XI (1833), *passim.*
4. *Ibid.,* pp. 252–253.
5. *American Quarterly Observer* (Boston), I (1833), 95–101.
6. *Emporium and True American* (Trenton, N.J.), May 25, 1838.
7. *Niles's Register* (Baltimore), September 5, 1835.
8. *New York Herald,* September 1, 1835.
9. *New York Commercial Advertiser,* October 12, 1835.
10. *Ibid.,* October 12, 1835.
11. *Ibid.,* April 10, 1832.
12. Quoted by the *Liberator* (Boston), October 1833.
13. *Albany Argus,* August 11, 1835.
14. *Ibid.,* January 7, 1837.
15. *North American Review* (Boston), XXXV (1832), 128–142.
16. *Ibid.,* XLI (1835), *passim.*
17. James K. Paulding, *Slavery in the United States* (New York, 1836), p. 281.
18. J. R. Burden, *Remarks of Dr. J. R. Burden of Philadelphia County in the Senate of Pennsylvania on the Abolition Question, February 18, 1838,* (Philadelphia, 1838), p. 9.
19. *Ibid.,* p. 10.

20. *National Trades Union,* August 16, 1834.

21. Paulding, *op. cit.,* p. 28.

22. *New York Evening Post,* September 20, 1831.

23. *Kennebec Weekly Journal* (Augusta, Me.), August 21, 1835.

24. *Ibid.,* September 30, 1831; October 12, 1832; May 12, 1833; September 11, 1833; and *passim.*

25. *Boston Transcript,* August 21, 1831.

26. *Eastern Argus* (Portland, Me.), August 11, 1835.

27. *New Jersey Journal* (Elizabethtown, N.J.), November 10, 1835.

28. *Newburyport Daily Herald* (Newburyport, Mass.), October 8, 1833.

29. *Ibid.,* October 8, 1833.

30. *Ibid.,* October 24, 1835.

31. *Ibid.,* November 24, 1837; May 22, 1838.

32. Samuel May Collection Tract #261 (Cornell University Library).

33. *Portsmouth Weekly Journal* (Portsmouth, N. H.), August 21, 1835.

34. *Pennsylvanian* (Philadelphia), August 24, 1835.

35. *North American Review,* XXXV (1832), 128–142.

36. *New York Herald,* December 13, 1836.

37. *Ibid.,* May 23, 1838.

38. *Knickerbocker Magazine,* XI (1838), 328.

39. *National Trades Union,* July 12, 1834.

40. *New York Evening Post,* August 7, 1833.

41. James F. Cooper, *The American Democrat,* (new ed.; New York, 1931), pp. 166–167.

42. David M. Reese, *Humbugs of New York* (New York, 1838), pp. 113–114.

43. John Quincy Adams, "Letter to Doctor Benjamin Waterhouse, October 15, 1835," quoted in Samuel F. Bemis, *John Quincy Adams and the Union* (New York, 1956), p. 329.

44. Claude M. Fuess, *The Life of Caleb Cushing* (2 vols., New York, 1923), I, 155.

45. *Boston Atlas,* January 19, 1838.

46. *Boston Transcript,* May 19, 1838.

47. *Liberator* (Boston), March 8, 1836. Garrison wrote a lengthy account of the proceedings. He cited numerous anti-abolitionist remarks made by many members of the Massachusetts legislature.

48. Samuel Eliot Morison, *The Life and Letters of Harrison Gray Otis, Federalist, 1765–1848* (2 vols., Boston, 1913), II, 273.
49. *Boston Transcript,* May 19, 1838. Every newspaper I examined carried the story that white women delegates to the convention were seen walking arm in arm with colored male delegates.
50. *Boston Atlas,* May 22, 1838.
51. *Ibid.,* September 11, 1838.
52. *New York Herald,* January 6, 1837; November 27, 1837.
53. *Ibid.,* October 27, 1835.
54. *Ibid.,* October 21, 1836.
55. *New York Evening Post,* July 8, 1834.
56. *Ibid.,* November 18, 1837.
57. *Ibid.,* April 25, 1833.
58. Russel Nye, *Fettered Freedom* (East Lansing, Michigan, 1949), *passim.*

5

———•———

The Churches Face
the Moral Crusade

The churches in America had to give more attention to
antislavery than did any other group or institution in the
country. The churches had to face the issues raised by the
antislavery movement, because a number of clergymen and
prominent lay leaders were abolitionists. The churches' attempts to find a satisfactory position on the question of
abolition, and the specific stands the various religious in-

stitutions took, tell a very special story of the place abolition had in the North of the 1830's. As we examine that
story, we will also trace the anti-abolitionist response in
more detail, and from an institutional rather than a thematic
point of view.

The abolitionist movement was, of course, largely based
on a religious foundation, and such antislavery leaders as
Theodore Weld and Arthur Tappan were also closely associated with many other church-sponsored reforms. Weld,
like most abolitionists, viewed antislavery as a moral awakening of the North to the immorality of slavery. Abolitionists regularly spoke before some church congregations, and
there were clergymen prominent in the antislavery ranks.
But, just as antislavery failed to attract any major support
among college presidents, newspaper and magazine editors,
prominent writers, or politicians, it also failed to win over
many prominent churchmen or to gain support from any of
the important religious sects or denominations. Considering the intensity of expressions of anti-abolitionist sentiments, the issues this raised in the North, and the abolitionists' claim that theirs was a moral crusade, it is not surprising that many churchmen rejected antislavery. Their rejection was based not only on the usual reasons of racism and
fear of disunion and violence, but also on the fear that antislavery would disrupt their religious institutions. This
widespread clerical anti-abolitionism is another indication
of the extent of northern anti-abolitionism and of the fears
the abolitionists unintentionally had raised.

Historians have described the schism of 1837 in the Presbyterian church as one of the first instances of an American institution dividing over the slavery question.[1] This claim, however, is misleading. The Presbyterian church split over doctrinal questions, questions that had been argued for a long time and that came to a head in 1837 in the midst of a great period of evangelical activity. Antislavery was important only as an element in this doctrinal debate. In order to understand the role of antislavery in this schism, we must consider the controversies within the church that led to the final split.

In 1801 the Presbyterian and Congregational churches, worried about the loss of membership as New Englanders moved West, joined together in a plan of union. Concerned for the salvation of those who were moving beyond the bounds of the established churches into areas where properly trained clergymen were unavailable, the church sent missionaries into the frontier region, and by the mid-1820's a wave of revivalism was sweeping western New York and the Western Reserve of Ohio. The missionaries conducting these revivals began to bring large numbers of people into the two churches, and hence the American Missionary Board, which controlled the funds for these actitivites, assumed an increasingly important place within the church structure.[2]

When Charles Grandison Finney turned to the ministry and, in the 1820's, had great success in conducting revivals, the more orthodox wings of both churches feared that the interdenominational missionary groups, which were closely associated with evangelism, would gain control of the church organization. Thus, they feared, Finney's new theology might subvert orthodox church doctrine. Perhaps the most dangerous part of the new doctrine, as the conservatives saw it, was typified by the preaching of the radical Presbyterian minister Albert Barnes. In a sermon entitled "The Way of Salvation," published in 1829 and violently attacked by both Old-School and more moderate New-School men, Barnes said of salvation, "No man has a right to conclude that he is shut out from salvation, *except by fact,* if he loves sin, and will not repent. . . . If *he* should repent and believe, as he would be saved and be among the elect, and give the glory to God." [3] Presbyterian leaders like Charles Hodge rejected any doctrine in which salvation was so simply attained, and which granted such easy admittance into the ranks of the elect.

As for the growing power of the Home Missionary Society, Hodge's Princeton colleague Samuel Miller spoke for the anti-evangelical Old-School Presbyterians when he wrote, in 1833, in his *Letters to Presbyterians on the Present Crisis in the Presbyterian Church:*

> Yet we all know that they [Board of American Home Missionary Society] have no public standards to which they engage to be conformed. They have no confession of faith; no ecclesiastical responsibility. They may deviate greatly and grievously from the purity of the gospel; and if this should ever occur there will be no other power than the vague and

ever varying power of public sentiment to call them to account or to arrest their wayward career.[4]

Moderates considered that the New-School (pro-evangelical) men, who were associated with interdenominational societies and in a few cases became abolitionists, would destroy the discipline of the church, since these reformers worked in societies outside the control of the Presbyterian General Assembly. Though few New-School men actually participated, abolition was the kind of crusade to which the revivalistic type of New-School theology might lead. Old-School men considered the participation of some New-School men in the abolitionist movement proof of the danger of evangelism.

In 1836 Charles Hodge, editor and chief contributor to the *Biblical Repertory and Theological Review,* a journal of the Theological Seminary at Princeton, stated:

> The assumption that slaveholding is itself a crime, is not only an error, but it is an error fraught with evil consequence. It not merely brings its advocates into conflict with the scriptures, but it does much to retard the progress of freedom: it embitters and divides the members of the community, and distracts the Christian Church.[5]

In 1838 Hodge said, when commenting on West Indian emancipation, that abolitionists were "fighting against scripture" and that "they consider their own light as more sure than the word set down in scripture." [6] Hodge considered this point crucial. The abolitionists, like the revivalists who sought to direct the activities of the church into associations for reform, failed to follow the literal statements of the Bible. Once the ministers were broadly interpreting the Bible, church discipline would break down. What to Hodge and the Old-School Presbyterians was radicalism would become dominant.

Aside from pointing to abolition as the worst consequence of evangelism, the *Biblical Repertory* neglected the subject. From 1831 to 1839 only three articles in the *Repertory* mentioned antislavery: the two already cited, and a note in favor of colonization published in 1833. This hardly seems the kind of coverage the principal organ of the Presbyterian church would give to an issue that threatened to divide the church.

On the question of evangelical activity, the opposition to Hodge and to the Princeton Old-School men came mainly from the evangelist Charles Finney and the group of reformers who had accepted his stand. Finney, though more sympathetic to abolition than the Old-School Presbyterians, refused to join the abolitionist movement.

In 1836, after his revivals had made him famous, Finney became president of Oberlin College, a college then controlled by New-School Presbyterians and a center of reform activity. Several of Oberlin's prominent faculty members had publicly supported antislavery, and the school had offered admittance to the students of Lane Seminary when they left that institution following their antislavery discussions. The Lane students, faculty members such as Beriah

Green and Presbyterian philanthropist and antislavery leader Lewis Tappan, sought to convince Finney to join the antislavery cause, but without success.[7]

Theodore Weld was among those evangelists who played an important role in carrying out the work of the American Anti-Slavery Society. Weld was a former disciple of Finney, and he too attempted to convince Finney to join the antislavery crusade. It was in answer to Weld's appeal that Finney wrote a letter explaining why he rejected abolition:

> Br. Weld is it not true, at least do you not fear it is, that we are in our present course going fast into a civil war? Will not our present movements in abolition result in that: . . . Nothing is more manifest to me than that the present movements will result in this unless your mode of abolitionizing the country be greatly modified. . . . How can we save our country and affect the speedy abolition of slavery? This is my answer. . . .
> The subject is now before the public mind. It is upon the conscience of every man, so that now every new convert will be an abolitionist of course. Now if abolition can be made an appeal of a general revival of religion all is well. I fear no other liberty of the soul of the slave. One alarming fact is that the absorbing abolitionism has drunk up the spirits of some of the most efficient moral men and is fast doing so [to] the rest, . . . This I have been trying to resist from the beginning as I have all along foreseen that should that take place, the church and world, ecclesiastical and state leaders, will become embroiled in one common infernal squabble that will roll a wave of blood over the land. The causes now operating are in my view as certain to lead to

this result as a cause is to produce effect, unless the public mind can be engrossed with the subject of salvation and make abolition an appendage of the revival in Rochester. . . . The fact is D [ear] W [eld] our leading abolitionists are good men, but there are but a few of them *wise* men.[8]

Finney considered reform possible only if men were awakened and made to see the evil around them. The spirit of religion would automatically produce antislavery advocates, but to pursue it as an objective apart from all others would be disastrous. He remained outside the antislavery movement because it differed from his idea of what a reform movement should be. Finney rejected abolition because it sought to destroy slavery by direct attack on that institution and the men who participated in it. For Finney, reform should be a spiritual awakening of the nation, not a crusade to change part of the fundamental social system— at least not as the first step. Though some of his followers did join, many stayed away.

There seems no reason to assume, as some historians have done, that the New-School Presbyterians were abolitionists. Some of them were; some were sympathetic to antislavery but not to abolition; others took no stand. In 1838 the New-School General Assembly met in Philadelphia and when a memorial on slavery was presented, the General Assembly insisted it be withdrawn. Meeting in 1839, the General Assembly declared that the question of slavery was outside its province.[9]

Only after 1850 did the New-School Assembly vote to regard slavery as "intrinsically an unrighteous and oppressive system opposed to the proscriptions of the law of God." [10] In 1839 the *American Biblical Repository,* journal of the New School, discussed the schism. The writer never mentioned antislavery.[11] Even a pro-abolitionist Presbyterian like Joshua Leavitt, editor of the *New York Evangelist,* indicated that his prime concern was that Presbyterians be active in reform; in the *Evangelist,* he devoted more space to other reforms than to antislavery.[12] In August 1837 Leavitt wrote, "We shall not make the abolition question the all absorbing topic, we shall not be men of one idea." [13]

Considering the stand taken by leaders of the Presbyterian church, we can assume that, although there were ministers of this denomination who preached abolitionist doctrines, the Presbyterian laity were, for the most part, not subject to such appeals. In October 1835, in a sermon entitled "A View of the American Slavery Question," the Reverend E. P. Barrows of the First Free Presbyterian Church of New York said, though he favored antislavery in principle, he felt it unfair to condemn slaveholders to the point of barring them from church membership, because the conditions under which emancipation might be accomplished were so difficult.[14]

The Reverend Gilbert McMaster of the Reformed Presbyterian Church in Duanesburgh, New York, published a sermon he had delivered in 1832 in which he said: abolition denied states' rights; slavery was an evil, but no worse than other evils sanctioned by the Constitution; slavery might be wrong but it would take a long time to correct it, and the slaveholders would be the ones to end the institution.[15]

The Dutch Reformed wing of the Presbyterian church adopted an even stronger anti-abolitionist position. The journal of the Dutch Reformed Church of New York, the *Christian Intelligence,* carried notices supporting colonization and the idea that the church's duty was to send missionaries to the Negroes in Africa. The editor made it clear that he felt a sense of duty to the Negro as an object for good works, but that Americans were opposed to incorporating Negroes into white society.[16] As another Dutch Reform journal put it, "Sinful as slavery is it is not more so than a plan of emancipation might be made to be." [17] In Philadelphia Ashabel Green, editor of the Presbyterian *Christian Advocate,* stated his dislike of slavery, his fear of abolition, and his support for colonization.[18]

These are only a few examples of statements by Presbyterian clergymen which indicate that clergy's opposition to abolition. Neither the Presbyterian church organization nor the interdenominational reform societies which Presbyterians and Congregationalists dominated were happy about any movement as potentially decisive as abolition.

The clergymen of the Congregationalist church were a college-trained group, strong in New England and areas where New Englanders had settled. With their closely associated Presbyterian brothers the Congregationalist clergy dominated the boards of directors of the various reform movements of the day. A number of historians have sought to establish that these clergymen "had a definite pattern for America to which they wanted the nation to conform." [19] These "theocrats," who were strongest among the New England Congregationalists, used reform movements to accomplish their ends.

Though the "theocrats" were associated with a variety of reform societies, their solution to the Negro problem was to support the American Colonization Society and to reject the idea that the Negro could be part of the American nation.[20] Ralph Gurley, secretary of the American Colonization Society, Samuel Mills, one of its founders, Robert Finley, another important figure in the founding of the Society, all were "theocrats." [21]

Among the leaders of the Congregational church, the New Englander Lyman Beecher serves as a good example of a "theocrat" who rejected abolition. The "theocrats" considered Andrew Jackson a special menace and had started a concerted drive in 1829 to awaken the country to the danger of oversecularism in government and society.[22] Though personal enemies, Beecher and Finney both believed their goal to be the preparation of Americans for the Second Coming. If this was accomplished, all reforms would follow. Beecher believed that to work for a particular and singled-out reform would only endanger the greater cause.[23]

In 1834 Beecher accepted a call to head the newly formed Lane Theological Seminary in Cincinnati. He went West to fight atheism and popery, forces which posed a threat to a moral America. At Lane, Beecher found himself in the middle of an antislavery controversy. Arthur Tappan, antislavery leader, backed Lane financially. In a letter to Tappan Beecher explained why he prohibited further discussion of abolition. Though the crux of his argument was that he wished to see slavery end, he felt the best means to accomplish this was to make it as easy as possible for slaveholders to manumit—colonization would do just that.[24]

After the Lane project collapsed, Beecher returned to Boston. There, as one of his reform projects, he established the American Union, a group claiming to stand for "moderate abolition." Beecher hoped the American Union would bring together abolitionists and colonizationists. The "theocrats" constantly faced dissension in the ranks and the antislavery debate threatened to create a divisive issue. Thus Beecher sought to close the fissure; but Garrison denounced the American Union as a Colonization Society front, and it failed in its purpose.[25] Beecher wrote to his son William in 1835: "I hope and believe that the abolitionists as a body will become more calm and less denunciatory, with the exception of the few he-goat men, who think they do God service by butting every thing in the line of their march which does not fall in or get out of the way.

99

They are the offspring of the Oneida denunciatory revivals." [26] But Beecher, who was now embroiled in doctrinal controversies, dropped the antislavery debate.

The "theocrats" continually had to reckon with the potential division that abolition might cause among them. In 1837 Lyman Beecher's daughter Catherine Beecher, who had been with him in Cincinnati, wrote a tract in which she further developed the American Union's arguments against the abolitionists. In *An Essay on Slavery and Abolitionism: Letters Addressed to Angelina Grimké*,[27] Catherine started out by chiding Miss Grimké, a Quaker abolitionist soon to be the wife of Theodore Weld, for taking part in the abolitionist movement. This, she asserted, was not the proper role for a woman.[28]

Miss Beecher addressed herself to the apparently growing success of the movement her father had rejected. She declared that the abolitionists' course could only lead to violence and that "It is not so much by exciting feelings of pity or humanity, and Christian love, towards the oppressed, the elements that made other reforms successful as it is by awakening indignation at the treatment of the abolitionists themselves that their cause has prospered." [29]

She went on to say that though the abolitionists had not done this purposely, it had happened. "The Christian way would have been to respect the opposition's ideas and argue rationally against them." [30] The abolitionists were so engrossed in their single cause, wrote Miss Beecher, that they became irresponsible in their attacks on all those who disagreed with them:

> Abolition tries to coerce rather than persuade public opinion. They claim to preach the truth but don't consider whether they are making the evil better or worse. They say they leave the consequences to God. What they must accept is that the propriety and duty of a given course is to be decided by *probabilities as to its results;* and these probabilities are to be determined by the *known laws of mind and the records of past experience.*
>
> For only one of two positions can be held. Either that it is the duty of all men to remonstrate at all times against all violations of duty, and leave the consequences with God; or else that men are to use their judgement, and take the part of remonstrance only at such time and place, and in such manner, as promise the best results. Slavery will come to an end. What is to be gained or lost by forcing immediatism? [31]

Miss Beecher then repeated that reform must come from within; she told the abolitionists that "reformers must first exempt themselves from fault, to learn humility and meekness. They must be discreet. They are teachers who must have the help of the parent." [32] To the Beechers abolition was a stumbling block in the way of reform, rather than a crusade to accomplish reform.

The opinions of the Beechers and other Congregationalist reformers were expressed in the pages of the *Boston Recorder,* a weekly newspaper. The *Recorder* supported a host of reform associations. On the question of slavery Calvin

Stowe, the paper's editor, reflected the view of most New England Congregationalists that the American Colonization Society provided the best answer.[33] William Lloyd Garrison made it a point to attack the *Recorder*'s stand on the slavery question. In answer, Stowe defended its colonizationalist position on the grounds that it would "save Africa" and that the purpose was more than just getting rid of Negroes. As to the question of whether slaveholders were sinners, the paper's stand was that reform associations should withhold judgment.[34] Shortly after Garrison had published *Thoughts on African Colonization,* in which he attacked the colonization principle, the *Recorder* published rejoinders.

By the mid-1830's the *Recorder* declared that corrupt men were using the antislavery societies, and that most of the members, who doubtless meant well, were being led astray. Following the riots of 1835, the paper noted, though the abolitionists did not intend slave insurrection their doctrines would produce it, and the abolitionists would be helpless to stop such violence just as they were helpless to stop anti-abolitionist riots in the North.[35]

Many Congregationalist clergymen in New England agreed with the *Recorder*'s stand on slavery, abolition, and colonization. We saw that Lyman Beecher, though he rejected abolition, did make an effort to bring about a compromise between colonization and antislavery. Another leading Congregationalist, Horace Bushnell, rejected any such compromise. Bushnell, who by 1839 had become a prominent clergyman in Connecticut, made very clear his opposition to an antislavery movement.[36] In January 1839 Bushnell discussed slavery before the congregation of the North Church in Hartford. He had spoken on the subject before but this was, in his words, a summing up of his views on the course of abolition. Bushnell's first objection to the abolitionists' doctrines was their harshness toward slaveholders. He found the claim that all slaveholders were sinners most disturbing:

> If our countrymen are guilty in this matter of slavery, it is not holding what they know to be truth concerning it—not doing what they are able, as individuals, properly enlightened, to produce a right action in their legislatures—and neglecting, in the meantime, to guard the well-being of their slaves by acts of parental and Christian kindness. That many of them incur great personal guilt in the matter is not to be questioned. But yet, when we speak of them, we ought to remember the fearfulness and difficulty of their state. Which way soever they turn, they meet the view of something dark or frightful.[37]

Bushnell exonerated slaveholders from the guilt of slavery by arguing that the present generation had inherited slavery and not created it. Southerners had been brought up in a society in which slavery was accepted. Slavery was a crime, but "if there was ever a people on earth involved in crime, who yet deserved sympathy and gentleness at the hand of the good, it is the slaveholding portion of our country." [38]

After describing the evils of slavery, evils that stemmed from the fact that slavery destroyed the sanctity of the home and prevented the individual from exercising proper control over his person, Bushnell appealed to the South:

> This institution is your own, not ours. Take your own way of proceeding. . . . Invent any new fashion of society you please. . . . But let me declare to you that, until you have established the family state and made it sacred, till you have given security to the body, till you have acknowledged the immortal mind and manhood of your slave, you do an offense to God and humanity. . . . In this sense, I am ready to go for the abolition of slavery.[39]

Bushnell then turned his attention to the abolitionists. He assured them that the moral position of the entire world was against slavery, that slavery was basically immoral and would be destroyed. But he also insisted that their program was the wrong way to bring reform: "either with you, or without you . . . the river flows inevitably—abolition may only muddy the water." [40] The Congregationalist based his analogy on the belief that the abolitionists, by calling for the acceptance of the Negro as an equal, held a false view of the Negro's capabilities and potentialities:

> The vision of a new created, enlightened race of Christian freemen, which they ever hold up before them [the abolitionists]. . . . I am sorry to feel, has too slender a support in history where an uncultivated and barbarous stock has been elevated in the midst of a cultivated and civilized stock. . . . The Irish for example can't really become

Americans. They become extinct. It is very seldom that their children, born in this country live to a mature age. Intemperance and poor living sweep them away.[41]

The Congregationalist clergy, as well as the members of other religious and secular groups in American society, represented a range of views on the issue of abolition, and most of them objected to it. A few Maine Congregationalist ministers called for support of abolition, but they met with a storm of criticism. Congregationalists there as elsewhere either supported the American Colonization Society, or were apologists for slavery.

For a time William Lloyd Garrison numbered among his supporters a group of Massachusetts Congregationalist ministers. By 1837, however, many of these ministers joined in attacking Garrison because he began associating the movement with women's rights.[42] These clergymen, however, advocated antislavery; but Lyman Beecher, Horace Bushnell, Leonard Bacon, and most of the leaders of the Congregational church stopped short of even nominal support of the abolitionist cause. Since the Congregationalists did not have a general conference, the church never formally debated the issue.

The Methodist church was organized into regional conferences, which were under the jurisdiction of the General Conference. Here the antislavery men had their chance to try to win over at least their regional conferences. The abolitionists were probably more numerous among northern Methodists than in any other denomination.[43] Yet, these antislavery advocates met strong opposition even in the New England, New Hampshire, and New York conferences where they were most prominent. The bishops of these conferences, without exception, exerted their influence and the power invested in them by the church to block the abolitionists.[44]

In the early 1820's the Methodists, leading the way in missionary activity both at home and overseas, decided to send a mission to the American Negro colony in Liberia. The church had strongly supported the American Colonization Society, and the mission brought even closer cooperation between the two. When, in the 1830's, abolitionists began a strong attack on the Colonization Society in New England, Bishops Hedding and Waugh, Professor Whedon of Wesleyan, and Doctor Fisk, who was the president of that college, all opposed the organized antislavery movement.

In several histories of the Methodist church, the long fight between the antislavery forces and the Methodist hierarchy has been discussed at length.[45] We shall consider here the nature of the anti-abolitionist sentiment that was so strong in the North.

The Methodist General Conference of 1836 met in Cincinnati, just across the Ohio River from the slave-state Kentucky. Cincinnati had a strong anti-abolitionist history dating from the violent opposition to the "Lane Rebels" who had sought to educate the city's free Negroes. And

James G. Birney, the future antislavery leader, faced mob action against his press and himself in 1836, soon after he began editing an antislavery journal.[46] Obviously, Cincinnati was an unfavorable location for those Methodist delegates from New England who came to the conference hoping to see an antislavery memorial read and some action taken.[47]

Several days before the conference opened, two of these delegates addressed a meeting of the local antislavery society. Once the conference sessions began, their activities were noted and a debate ensued on the question of censuring them. The debate resulted in a resolution disapproving of "the most unqualified members of the General Conference who are reported to have lectured in this city recently upon, and in favor, of modern abolitionism."

It was traditional for the assembly to open with an address from a representative of the Methodist Church of England. This English representative now joined with the antislavery delegates. In his address he called on the Americans to oppose slavery. The assembly opposed this invitation and declared they were "decidedly opposed to modern abolitionism, and wholly disclaim any right, wish, or intention, to interfere in the civil and political relation between master and slave as it exists in the slaveholding states of the Union." [48] One speaker then pointed out, for the benefit of the English delegate, that there were important differences between the problems of abolishing slavery in England and abolishing it in the United States. Other speakers condemned abolition and called it almost as dangerous a conspiracy as Catholicism.[49]

Though the Methodist antislavery men got nowhere in Cincinnati, they had at least forced debate on the slavery question and had put the official church bodies on the defensive there, as they had already succeeded in doing in the New England Conference.

Orange Scott and La Roy Sunderland, who led the New England Methodist antislavery group, found that opposi-Conference would make it impossible for the antislavery wing to express its views in the Methodist press. Therefore, tion by the bishops and other prominent churchmen of the Sunderland established his own paper in New York, the *Zion's Watchman.* In this paper Methodist antislavery men now expressed their views. When, in 1835, the paper published an appeal to all Methodist clergymen to join the cause of antislavery, Wesleyan's Professor Whedon wrote a "Counter-Appeal," which was signed by President Fisk of that college, and by Edward Taylor, Abel Stevens, and five other leaders of the New England conference.[50]

A "Pastoral Letter" addressed to "The Ministers and Preachers of the New England and New Hampshire Conferences" and signed by Bishops Hedding and Emory followed the "Counter-Appeal." In the letter the bishops declared: "Nothing has ever occurred so seriously tending to obstruct and retard, if not absolutely to defeat, the cause of emancipation as the modern agitation on this subject." [51]

They called upon all presiding elders, preachers, trustees, and members to manifest their disapprobation and to refuse the abolitionists the use of their pulpits. When approached to sign a petition against slavery in the District of Columbia, Fisk, president of Wesleyan, refused.[52] In Methodist regional conferences, Hedding, Fisk, and Waugh of New York all exerted their full prerogative to cut off abolitionist petitions and to prevent antislavery debate. In 1838, in the Maine and New York conferences, it was voted to end all discussion of the slavery question.[53] Luther Lee, an abolitionist leader in the Methodist church, was refused the right to speak from a Methodist pulpit in Auburn, New York.[54] Clearly, the Methodist leadership had little sympathy for the abolitionist cause.

Though there were some abolitionists in the northern conferences, most Methodists were anti-abolitionist. The anti-abolitionists were in complete control in all but two conferences, those of New Hampshire and New England, and in all northern conferences the leading figures, bishops, and ministers, stood opposed to antislavery. The revolt of antislavery Methodists resulted from their failure to win over their church.

The Baptists, like the Methodists, had to contend with an English church group that was pressuring them to take an antislavery stand. And like the Methodists, the Baptists' answer showed conclusively that even in the northern churches abolitionism was unpopular.

Baptists sympathetic to antislavery claimed the sect had

a tradition of antislavery that extended all the way back to Roger Williams. Williams had spoken out against the slave trade and had freed Indian slaves in Rhode Island. In the late eighteenth century the church had come out in favor of gradual abolition of slavery, and in the early nineteenth century a group known as the Friends of Humanity, most of whom lived west of the Alleghenies, had taken up antislavery as one of their causes.[55] During the 1830's, however, few Baptists were actually willing to support antislavery.

The English Baptists had been among the leaders in securing freedom of all slaves held in the Empire. Once this was accomplished, they turned their attention to the American scene. In December of 1833 church leaders wrote a letter to their American brethren urging them to take an antislavery stand. After waiting some time (abolitionists claimed the delay was actually an attempt to keep the letter a secret), the American Baptist Convention answered their English critics.[56] The spokesmen for the Convention began by insisting abolition was far more difficult in America than in England. First, the Convention's spokesman pointed out the difference in political structure between the United States and Great Britain, a difference which made it possible for Parliament to legislate for the whole Empire on the subject of slavery, while in the United States the federal system made it necessary for each state to handle the problem. One state could not interfere with another. This was what the Constitution provided, and the Union could be preserved only if Americans followed the dictates of the Constitution. Thus, the Convention spokesman pointed out, slavery existed before the Revolution and had in fact been introduced to Americans by the British.[57]

Next, the American Baptist noted that the large number of slaves in America made immediate emancipation impossible. "It is not believed by many of the sincere friends of the slaves, that their immediate emancipation would be conducive to their own real welfare, or consistent with the safety of the whites. . . . Slaves who have regarded labour as an irksome task can have little idea of liberty, except as an exemption from toil." [58] The Baptist spokesman emphasized that he opposed the immediate emancipation of slaves but that he was willing to defend the American Colonization Society. Baptist missionary groups were especially strong supporters of colonization.

Third, the spokesman for the American Baptist Convention, writing in Boston, pointed out the dangers to Baptist church unity if the Convention took a strong antislavery stand. The Baptists, like the Methodists, had a large southern membership. The writer made clear to his English associates the importance of maintaining friendly relations:

There is now a pleasing degree of union among . . . Baptists throughout the land. . . . Southern Baptists were liberal and zealous in promoting holy enterprises. Most are slaveholders but because the institution had firm root before they were born.[59]

Some months after this letter was written, a two-man delegation from the English church arrived in America. The delegates, Reverend F. A. Cox and Reverend J. Hoby, were antislavery advocates. Cox and Hoby addressed the Baptist Triennial Convention and toured the West and South. After returning to England, they wrote about their trip and provided a survey of the church in America.[60]

The two ministers began by telling their English audience that though they were abolitionists, they had kept quiet on the subject because "Americans are jealous of foreign interference; of all foreigners who intermeddle in their internal policy, they are most jealous of the English." [61] On no subject was this feeling so strong as on antislavery. The antislavery elements in the Baptist church tried to induce the two men at least to attend their meetings, but Cox and Hoby refused. Antislavery sympathizers in America claimed their refusal resulted from pressure from the executive board of the Triennial Convention. This the Englishmen denied, saying that they disagreed with some of the doctrines set forth by American abolitionists and felt their presence at a meeting would make it seem as though they sanctioned all antislavery ideas.[62] Whichever was the case, it seemed most expedient to these English observers to avoid taking a strong antislavery stand, even in the North.

The Baptist leaders in the North, like those of the other major denominations, expressed a dislike for slavery, but also a fear that abolition meant immediate freedom for the slave who, they believed, was unprepared for it. Many of these clergymen asserted their belief that it was impossible to mix Negroes and whites peacefully, and hence they supported colonization.

Francis Wayland, president of Brown University, was among the American Baptist leaders who expressed their views on the responsibility of the church with regard to the slavery question. In 1838 Wayland published a book entitled *The Limitations of Human Responsibility* in which he attacked the abolitionists and questioned the whole tendency toward what he called associationalism. First, Wayland remarked that true reform resulted from conscience directed by moral impulse. But one had to be very careful to distinguish what was true moral impulse. He warned that men who joined reform movements were often guided by the impulse of others, and this impulse might be false.[63] "Men plead the authority of God whilst they violate law; whilst they infringe the rights of their neighbor against infringement; whilst the individual takes the power of society into his own hands, and whilst society punishes him for transgression." [64] Wayland told his audience that they must not assume responsibility for all things. He then illustrated his point by describing the dangers inherent in a variety of associational forms, among which was antislavery.[65]

Agreeing that slavery was a moral wrong, Wayland asked what the Baptists' duty was with respect to it. How were American Baptists limited in their actions with regard to slavery? He gave his answer in two parts. As citizens of the United States, he said, American Baptists had certain limitations as to action, and as human beings under God's law they were also limited. In discussing the former, he emphasized that the Constitution, by recognizing slavery, was actually a legal restraint. As to the Baptists' limitations as human beings, Wayland made the point that they must respect the rights of fellow human beings in the South. To support abolition would be to support those who would start a servile war. The Baptist leader claimed that the abolitionists had fallen prey to the weakness of many another association, for they had allowed their movement to be taken over by a few "third-rate politicians." He accused the abolitionists of fanaticism for no good purpose and stated that they had actually riveted the slaves' bonds tighter.[66] Wayland's final advice to his readers was individually to speak the truth and hope that men's consciences would lead them to accept it.[67] As an important figure in the Baptist church as well as a recognized scholar and writer, Wayland carried much weight among Baptists.

Other Northern Baptist leaders agreed with Wayland. In 1834 A. A. Phelps, a Congregationalist minister and for a time editor of the American Anti-Slavery Society newspaper the *Emancipator,* formulated a declaration urging immediate emancipation; only 11 Baptist ministers in New England and New York signed it.[68] The leaders of the Baptist church, like those of the Methodists, avoided association with the antislavery movement, while some of these leaders attacked the abolitionists.

The Episcopal church, like so many other denominations, was faced with the problem of taking a stand on the question of engagement in evangelist activities. In upstate New York the church undoubtedly felt the impact of Charles Finney's evangelist efforts. Throughout the late 1820's and into the 1830's Bishop Hobart of New York was engaged in a fight with other Episcopalian church leaders over the issue of evangelism, and the use of evangelist methods by Episcopal ministers. In the Episcopal church, however, even those who held evangelist doctrines rejected the anti-slavery movement. The church either avoided the subject or attacked antislavery. Calvin Colton, who left newspaper work to become an Episcopal clergyman and then gave up the Church for politics, was an outspoken critic of the abolitionist. In a tract written in 1836 Colton attacked all reform associations for giving too much power, through their centralized organization, to the men who led them. Such groups, Colton warned, were bound to get involved in politics, which was not the proper realm of action for churchmen. Colton attacked the whole revivalist trend that was then so strong in many denominations.[69]

In 1839, in his book entitled *Abolition a Sedition* Colton pointed out how abolition was associated with "violent reforms that threatened good social order."[70] As he had warned in 1836, abolitionists had gone into politics. Now he accused them of being an independent (thus uncontrolled) group that both threatened the Union and sought the overthrow of the government. Here was a religious group seeking to subvert the state. He concluded his remarks with the usual anti-abolitionist advice to the British, telling them to mind their own business.[71]

Colton's skepticism about reform was shared by other Episcopal leaders. In 1837 the Episcopal diocese of New York began the publication of a magazine entitled the *New York Review and Quarterly Church Journal.* In July 1838 the *Review,* spurred by the publication of Harriet Martineau's *Society in America,* expressed its views on the slavery question and on the whole subject of reform. The editor, though he accepted the idea of man's potential perfectibility, asked his readers to remember that there is in man a radically corrupt tendency that must be restrained. This, he continued, the perfectionists forgot when they called for even more freedom for the individual. For example, a person might believe the end of slavery desirable but not realize that the problem lies in finding some way to end it. As Miss Martineau wrote of race hatred in America, the editor felt prompted to ask how, if the races hated each other one could expect them to live together in peace, without slavery to govern their relations? [72]

In the next issue, in a review of Francis Wayland's *Limitations of Human Responsibility,* the editor pursued the same theme. The Episcopal journal quoted Wayland at length, taking special note of his views on abolition in such statements as the following:

They [the abolitionists] have raised a violent agitation, without presenting any definite means of constitutionally accomplishing their objective. In the meantime, as combination on the one side always produces combinations on the other, they have embittered the feelings of the South. They have for the present, at least, rendered any open and calm discussion of the subject in the slaveholding states, utterly impossible. They have riveted indefinitely, the bond of the slave. . . . I must come to the conclusion that their efforts must be unwisely directed or else, they would have led to a more salutatory result.[73]

The reviewer praised Wayland's book and indicated that he agreed completely with his views.[74]

The Lutheran church, like the Episcopal church, had to deal with an evangelical wing interested in reform movements. The Lutheran reformers were centered in upstate New York. There were a few, but very few, antislavery men among these Lutherans. In 1836 the Hartwick Synod in New York State split over the question of whether the church should engage in evangelical activities. The Franckean Synod was formed by a handful of Lutheran ministers who sought to bring the church into reform movements. Though they supported abolition, they broke with the church for reasons other than their stand on slavery; antislavery was just one of many reforms they supported. But the great majority of Lutherans thought it improper for an ecclesiastical body to discuss the abolition of slavery or other reforms, or to participate in such activities.[75]

The Unitarian church took the position that slavery in the abstract was an evil, but that immediate abolition would be a grave error. The Unitarian *Christian Examiner and General Review* supported the Colonization Society.[76] The editor, pointing out how Africans in America were degraded, remarked that blacks should be allowed to stay if they wished, though their going to Africa would be best for both races. The *Examiner* called for the gradual extinction of slavery and warned that Garrison's plans would produce too rapid a social change: the French Revolution provided evidence of the danger of such change.[77]

William Ellery Channing was a reformer who rejected reform movements. Channing was convinced that all men were equal in that all had the same opportunity of infinite improvement of themselves; he considered such improvement a matter of personal concern and not the object of group crusade.[78] It is not surprising that this New England Unitarian would reject the appeals for his membership in the New England Anti-Slavery Society. But Channing chose to say a good deal more about his reasons for refusing to join an antislavery society. His pronouncements on abolition provide interesting insights into the reasons why many humanitarian-minded northerners rejected what seems on the surface the most humanitarian of causes.

Channing considered the abolitionists living proof of why reform must be achieved through the working of personal conscience rather than through outside group pressuring. In 1837, following the murder of abolitionist editor Elijah Lovejoy, Channing wrote that when "an enterprise of Christian Philanthropy" leads to and is involved in the use of force it is time to stop. Abolitionists must not pursue their objective if it means "wading through blood." [79] In the same letter Channing reprimanded the abolitionists for claiming that slaveholders disqualified themselves from church membership. The Unitarian leader considered such attacks on slaveholders as entirely apart from the true spirit of reform and lacking in compassion for the sinner who in time can be saved.

Guided by his definition of reform, Channing had supported the idea that abolition of slavery was a state matter. If the abolitionists had their way, he argued, race war would result. While abolitionists and reformers had succeeded in making the public aware of the "horrors of slavery," Channing wrote, they had also opened discussions of the dangers of immediate emancipation. And the result of antislavery efforts was that the public now sought to avoid discussing the question. Thus, Channing argued, abolitionists had done more to delay emancipation than to speed it up.[80] The antislavery leader Samuel May had good reason to complain:

> All the objections, Doctor Channing alleged against us . . . were the common current objections of that day, hurled at us in less seemly phrases from the press, the platform and the pulpit. . . . It was sad that a man of such a mind and heart as Doctor Channing's could have thought them of sufficient importance to press them upon us as he did.[81]

Despite his objections to the abolitionists, by the end of the decade Channing assumed a position very close to theirs. In 1838 he declared it the moral duty of the North to do something about slavery: a virtual about-face from his earlier stand when he had insisted that it was the duty of the South alone to act. Channing joined the abolitionists in denouncing the annexation of Texas on the grounds that it was a southern move to perpetuate slavery, and he spoke often now of the need to protect the abolitionists' civil rights, attacked colonization, and denied that the abolitionist plan meant amalgamation of the races.[82] However, Channing still refused to join the movement or to support it publicly.

Among the leaders of the Catholic church the dominant view was that slavery as an institution should be let alone, though interest was expressed in bringing religion to the slaves. Bishop Kendrick of Philadelphia asserted that slavery was an old and necessary institution, and that the proper concern of the church was with souls and not with the changing or even challenging of institutions.[83] Faced as they were with widespread anti-Catholic sentiment, it seems likely that church leaders would have avoided an unpopular stand even had they been inclined to oppose slavery.

To this point I have neglected to mention the denomination most often cited as a staunch exponent of antislavery doctrines—the Quakers, with their long tradition of humanitarian activities. They have been left until last in order to bring out clearly the great weight of anti-abolitionist sentiment in the North.

As the Quakers were always prominent among the leaders of the American antislavery movement, most historians have overlooked that many Quakers held slaves. Though many Quaker meetings discussed slavery during the seventeenth and early eighteenth centuries, that institution was neither formally rejected, nor were Quaker slaveholders forced to dispose of their slaves.[84] From the early to the mid-eighteenth century the Quakers, after years of persecution and schism, were seeking unity and were reluctant to risk a split on the slavery issue. They disowned two antislavery radicals, William Southeby and John Farmer, and when Ralph Sandiford and Benjamin Lay sought to revive the crusade in the 1730's, the Philadelphia Quakers took steps to silence them. However, by the late eighteenth century the Society of Friends was turning more markedly toward antislavery.[85]

In the 1730's Quakers began freeing their slaves, and by 1808 the process was complete. During the same period they also were working for the abolition of slavery as a whole. After 1800, with the measure outlawing the slave trade passed and the early leaders gone, the Quakers turned to testimony against slavery and little more.[86] We have already seen how the Pennsylvania Abolition Society, which was dominated by Quakers, ceased its yearly meeting and decreased its activities markedly.

The Quakers, like other religious groups, were divided

over the question of evangelism. A few of the "Orthodox" and some "Hicksites," as the competing groups were called, expressed antislavery views, but neither group was predominantly in favor of abolition.[87] Some "Hicksites" did propose that slavery be attacked by refusing to use slave-made goods. The free-produce movement was inspired by a Quaker drive to boycott goods made by warring nations.[88] However, the Quakers never officially sanctioned such action. There were free-produce stores in Philadelphia, New York, and Boston advertising their wares in the *Liberator* but the movement never became widespread.

Although the Quakers reached the point of refusing to take any slaveholder into membership and provided the antislavery movement with leadership, it would still be inaccurate to say that, by the 1830's, the Quakers were strongly pro-abolitionist. In fact, as we shall see, they were quite strongly opposed to "modern abolition."

The Quakers had allowed some Negroes into membership, but Negroes had to sit on special benches when they attended the meeting. Quaker leader Anthony Benezet favored some scheme of colonization. In 1816, when the American Colonization Society was founded, it received support from many Friends. Benjamin Lundy, who for years led the antislavery movement and who introduced Garrison to the cause, never favored immediate emancipation and sought for a long time to improve colonization schemes. By the late 1820's Quakers, preoccupied with the "Hicksite" controversy and disturbed by the "radicalism" of those abolitionists who called for immediatism, began to withdraw from the antislavery movement. The Baltimore Friends Anti-Slavery Society was disbanded in 1829; in Philadelphia the Free Produce Movement was dropped. As Thomas Drake put it in *Quakers and Slavery in America:*

> The real problem for the Friends . . . lay in the fact that the line between slavery and antislavery which the new doctrine of immediatism drew left no ground on which Quakers could comfortably stand. They had led the country to the point where gradual measures had become suspect in the South and had ceased to satisfy many conscience reformers in the North. They had converted a new generation to antislavery but a generation impatient with the mildness and slowness of the Quaker way. Friends faced the alternative of recasting their anti-slavery testimony and technique, or withdrawing from the vanguard of the anti-slavery ranks.[89]

The Quakers, for the most part, preferred to avoid antislavery.

Radicals like Arnold Buffum and poet John Greenleaf Whittier joined Garrison in the New England Anti-Slavery Society, but they were a distinct minority in the Quaker group. In 1839 William Bassett, a Quaker of Lynn, Massachusetts, wrote a pamphlet in which he took a strong antislavery stand. For this, Bassett was ostracized from the Lynn meeting house and from the Society of Friends.[90] By 1833 Philadelphia Quakers were stating that participation in radical activities that would lead to excitement and violence would cause damage to their faith. Gradually, north-

ern meetings broke off association with antislavery societies. Northern Quakers refused to allow meeting houses to
be used for outside lectures. This injunction was partly responsible for the abolitionists' decision to build Pennsylvania Hall in Philadelphia; many Quakers saw in the burning
of the Hall proof of what might result from association
with the antislavery societies.[91]

Presbyterians, Congregationalists, Baptists, Methodists,
Episcopalians, Lutherans, Unitarians, Catholics, and Quakers—all took stands that placed the majority of their clerical leaders in opposition to the antislavery movement. The
northern public heard few antislavery sermons. They read
or at least were aware that their church leaders countered
the arguments when antislavery men within their
denominations did write or speak.

Once again, we must keep in mind that this does not
mean that the churches in question were dominated by pro-
slavery elements. While there certainly were clergymen
who felt religious groups should avoid the question, there
were others who attacked slavery but rejected abolition.
Northern churchmen expressed all these views.

NOTES

1. See C. Bruce Staiger, "Abolitionism and the Presbyterian Schism of
1837-8," *Mississippi Valley Historical Review*, XXXVI (December
1949), 391-414. Staiger shows how the question of whether the
Church should engage in evangelistic activity was a divisive issue

long before slavery became an issue. However, he believes that it was the slavery issue that caused the final schism. It is my belief that too few of the important Presbyterian clergymen were sympathetic to antislavery, for this issue to have led to any major schism.

2. Presbyterian or Congregational clergymen dominated such interdenominational associations as the American Home Missionary Society, the American Tract Society, and the Sunday School Union, as well as many societies with more secular aims. For an interesting discussion of the relation of these clergymen to such societies, see Clifford L. Griffin, "Religious Benevolence as Social Control 1815–1860," *Mississippi Valley Historical Review,* LIV (December 1957), 423–444.

3. Quoted by M. W. Armstrong, Lefferts A. Loetscher, and C. A. Anderson, eds., *The Presbyterian Enterprise: Sources of American Presbyterian History* (Philadelphia, 1956), pp. 147–148.

4. Quoted by Clifford M. Drury, *Presbyterian Panorama* (Philadelphia, 1952), pp. 147–148.

5. *Biblical Repertory and Theological Review,* VIII (1836), 298.

6. *Ibid.,* X (1838), *passim.*

7. Lewis Tappan, Beriah Green, and a number of the Lane students wrote to Weld criticizing Finney. See Gilbert Barnes and Dwight Dumond, eds., *Letters of Theodore Dwight Weld, Angelina Grimké Weld and Sarah Grimké* (New York, 1934), I, *passim.*

8. *Ibid.,* I, 320–323.

9. *Presbyterian Enterprise,* p. 164.

10. *Ibid.,* p. 165.

11. *Ibid.,* p. 148.

12. *New York Evangelist.* I read all issues published from 1835 to 1837.

13. *Ibid.,* VIII (August 5), 1837.

14. E. P. Barrows, *A View of the American Slavery Question* (New York, 1836), *passim.*

15. Gilbert McMaster, *The Moral Character of Civil Institutions of the United States* (Duanesburgh, N. Y., 1832), *passim.*

16. *Christian Intelligencer* (New York), April 8, 1837. Americans' conviction, that they, as a superior people, were obliged to help inferior people, constituted an important element in the missionary impulse. Supporters of missionary work viewed their cause as national as well as theological.

17. *Religious Monitor and Evangelical Repository* (Albany), VII (1830–1831), 35.
18. *Christian Advocate* (Philadelphia), XI (1834), 568.
19. John R. Bodo, *The Protestant Clergy and Public Issues 1812–1848* (Princeton, N. J., 1954), preface, viii. See also Griffin, "Religious Benevolence," and Richard L. Power, "A Crusade to Extend Yankee Culture," *The New England Quarterly*, XII (December 1940), for discussions of theocracy.
20. See Charles Cole, *The Social Ideas of the Northern Evangelists* (New York, 1954), p. 162.
21. Bodo, *op. cit.,* pp. 123–124.
22. Charles I. Foster, *An Errand of Mercy: The Evangelical United Front, 1790–1837* (Chapel Hill, N. C., 1960), p. 179.
23. Constance M. Rourke, *Trumpets of Jubilee* (New York, 1927), p. 73.
24. Lynian Beecher, *Autobiography and Correspondence* Charles Beecher, ed.(2 vols., New York, 1865), II, 323.
25. Garrison devoted several editorials to denouncing the American Union as a front for the Colonization Society.
26. L. Beecher, *op. cit.,* 345.
27. Catherine Beecher, *An Essay on Slavery and Abolitionism* (Philadelphia, 1837).
28. Initially the Grimké sisters were hesitant to make public appearances. When they did begin lecturing in support of antislavery, they added feminism as another cause to support. Feminism was classed with abolition as a radical reform, a dangerous movement aimed at upsetting society. Garrison also supported feminism and so further cemented the relation, in the public mind, between these two reforms.
29. *Ibid.,* pp. 12–14, 35–36.
30. *Ibid.,* p. 38.
31. *Ibid.,* pp. 44–45.
32. *Ibid.,* p. 145.
33. The Congregational church journal *Quarterly Register of the American Education Society* (Boston) noted that "all the important Ecclesiastical Bodies in the country . . . have expressed a decided friendship for its plans." III (1831), 61.
34. *Boston Recorder,* August 31, 1831; January 30, 1833.

35. *Ibid.*, August 7, 1835.
36. In 1841 Bushnell was offered the presidency of Congregationalist Middlebury College.
37. Horace Bushnell, *A Discourse on the Slavery Question Delivered in the North Church, Hartford, Connecticut, January 10, 1839* (Hartford, 1839), pp. 5–6.
38. *Ibid.*, p. 6.
39. *Ibid.*, p. 8.
40. *Ibid.*, p. 11.
41. *Ibid.*, p. 11.
42. In "the Clerical Appeal" a group of Congregationalists, who belonged to the New England Anti-Slavery Society, attacked Garrison's methods and his associating abolition with women's rights.
43. More Methodist ministers, Garrison claimed, supported antislavery than clergymen of any other denomination.
44. Crawford Barclay, *Early American Methodism* (New York, 1949), II, 83–84.
45. See Charles B. Swaney, *Episcopal Methodism and Slavery* (Boston, 1926); John N. Norwood, *The Schism in the Methodist Episcopal Church* (Alfred, N. Y., 1923); Barclay, *Early American Methodism*.
46. Upon leaving the American Colonization Society to join the American Anti-Slavery Society, Birney moved to Cincinnati and began publishing an antislavery journal. An anti-abolitionist mob forced him to leave the city for a time. See Betty Fladeland, *James Birney: Slaveholder and Abolitionist* (Ithaca, N.Y., 1955), *passim.*
47. Norwood, *op. cit.,* p. 30.
48. *Debate on Modern Abolitionism in the General Conference of the Methodist Episcopal Church* (Cincinnati, 1836), *passim.*
49. *Loc. cit.*
50. Barclay, *op. cit.,* 104.
51. *Ibid.*, 105.
52. Swaney, *op. cit.,* p. 48.
53. *Ibid.*, p. 73.
54. *Ibid.*, p. 106.
55. For an account of the activities of the Friends of Humanity see Joseph M. Shea, "The Baptists and Slavery, 1840–1845" (unpublished Master's dissertation, Clark University, 1933).
56. *Baptist Magazine* (London), January 1835, p. 8.

57. *Loc. cit.*
58. *Loc. cit.* Cox was a member of the British Anti-Slavery Society. He failed to attend the American Society meeting because American Baptist leaders convinced him that it would be best if he avoided any contact with American abolitionists. In England George Thompson denounced Cox, calling him a coward for yielding to pressure and being frightened away from the abolitionists because they were unpopular.
59. *Loc. cit.*
60. F. A. Cox and J. Hoby, *The Baptist in America* (New York, 1836), *passim.*
61. *Ibid.,* p. 101.
62. *Ibid.,* pp. 101–102.
63. Francis Wayland, *Limitations of Human Responsibility* (Boston, 1838), p. 4.
64. *Ibid.,* p. 10.
65. *Ibid.,* p. 13.
66. *Ibid.,* pp. 162, 173.
67. *Ibid.,* p. 170.
68. A. A. Phelps, *Lectures on Slavery and Its Remedy,* quoted by Barclay, *op. cit.,* II, 102.
69. Calvin Colton, *Thoughts on the Religious State of the Country with Reasons for Prefering the Episcopacy* (New York, 1836), p. 95.
70. Calvin Colton, *Abolition a Sedition* (Philadelphia, 1839), pref.
71. *Ibid.,* p. 106.
72. *New York Review and Quarterly Church Journal,* III (1838), 130–132.
73. *Ibid.,* 394.
74. *Loc. cit.*
75. The Lutheran church was split by a conflict between those who wished to Americanize the church and those who wished to retain the old-world forms and doctrines. The Hartwick Synod encompassed much of upstate New York and some of western New England. This synod favored Americanizing, which meant, among other things, turning to evangelist activities; this led to debate within the church and the synod. See Harry J. Kreider, *History of the United Lutheran Synod of New York and New England* (Philadelphia, 1954), I, 92–102; Robert Fortenbaugh, "American

Lutheran Synods and Slavery, 1830–1860," *Journal of Religion,* vol. XIII (January 1933).

76. *Christian Examiner and General Review* (Boston), XIII (1833), 108.

77. *Ibid.,* (1833), 308; XXVI (1839), 304–307.

78. For the best expositions of Channing's views see David P. Edgell, *William Ellery Channing: An Intellectual Portrait* (Boston, 1955); and Madeline Rice, *Federal Street Pastor* (New York, 1962).

79. William Ellery Channing, *A Letter to the Abolitionists* (Boston, 1837), p. 5.

80. William Ellery Channing, *Slavery* (Boston, 1835), p. 118.

81. Samuel May, *Recollections of the Anti-Slavery Conflict* (Cambridge, Mass., 1869), p. 185.

82. In a letter to Jonathan Phillips, published in Boston in 1839, Channing continued to defend the abolitionists' civil rights, but he insisted he was not sympathetic to their cause.

83. Joseph D. Brokhage, *Francis Patrick Kendrick's Opinions on Slavery,* (Washington, D. C., 1955), p. 237.

84. Thomas E. Drake, *Quakers and Slavery in America* (New Haven, 1950), pp. 22, 32.

85. *Ibid.,* pp. 39–48.

86. *Ibid.,* p. 112.

87. *Ibid., passim.* The discussion of Quaker doctrinal controversies was drawn from this work.

88. The *Liberator* carried advertisements for goods sold in free produce stores, and Garrison occasionally urged subscribers to patronize these stores.

89. Drake, *op. cit.,* p. 132.

90. *Letter from William Bassett, Lynn, Massachusetts, 1839;* reprinted as an antislavery tract by the American Anti-Slavery Society.

91. I found evidence that antislavery societies were unpopular in Philadelphia as early as 1823. In that year Governor Coles of Illinois, fearing that his state might fall under pro-slavery influence, wrote to his friend Nicholas Biddle asking for aid. Biddle referred Coles to a wealthy Quaker merchant and philanthropist, Roberts Vaux. Biddle told Coles not to mention that he got help from Vaux, because Vaux did not wish to be associated with the antislavery movement. Biddle wrote: "The abolition Society of this city had been the subject, whether justly or not I am unable to determine, of

much hostility at a distance, and would be rather injurious than beneficial to have it supposed that the society was active in the cause which you are supporting." See "Cole Letters," *Journal of Negro History*, III (April 1918), 158–195.

92. Drake, *op. cit.*, pp. 157–158.

6

———————•———————

Abolition and the
Anxieties of an Age

Anti-abolitionism was widespread and intense in the North of the 1830's. It was founded on the prejudice of racism and the belief that the antislavery movement encouraged foreign criticism of America and even outright foreign interference. The grave charge made by opponents of abolition was that the movement threatened the Union, the Constitution, the right of states to govern their own affairs, and that it could lead to violence and race war. Quite unintentionally, the abolitionists had raised and aggravated a whole series of basic and complex issues. The fears and passions which these issues aroused dominated anti-abolitionism; consequently, the northern objections to antislavery were not only far-reaching—extending to every geographical area and segment of society—but also often more emotional than rational. This concluding chapter will be an attempt to explain these issues and their significance for the anti-abolitionist response.

The twentieth century has been called an age of anxiety. Critics of this view have often noted that all ages are times of anxiety. Certainly, men have always experienced concern but anxiety seems to diminish at some times and grow at others, and its impact on the course of events seems greater at one time than another. It is important, however, to remember that both confidence and anxiety may become more intense in the same society and at the same time, for optimism about the future may be coupled with deep fears.

This combination of confidence and anxiety showed itself in the 1830's, in a confidence in America's ability to absorb immigrants as long as they were white Protestants—and in a fear that Catholics neither could nor wished to be absorbed, and in an anxious conviction that Negroes were incapable of becoming part of American society. Americans, in the 1830's, felt an intense nationalism, yet a concern about the increased power of the national government; a confidence in the future of the Union, but concern for its future should major problems be raised; a confidence in the strength and superiority of America in relation to Europe, but a constant fear of foreign conspiracy; a recognition of the great economic development of the country, combined with a fear of rapid economic change. Americans believed social evils could be eradicated, but they feared that God intended for men always to face evil in their world.[1]

The abolitionists raised or aggravated problems which in one way or another touched upon all these sources of fear and confidence. To begin with, there was a racial problem in the North; even though slavery had ended, there existed profound and obvious inequalities and antagonisms between the races. A few anti-abolitionists considered racism in America to be a reason for rejecting antislavery, but most anti-abolitionists were racists who took Negro inferiority for granted and so rejected (as totally impractical) any antislavery proposal that did not include colonization. Charles Finney and William Ellery Channing objected to abolition not because they were racists but because so many other northerners were. They feared that adding freed slaves to the northern Negro population would intensify already existing problems. This was a rational perception of a real difficulty. But it is evident that anti-abolitionism also drew much strength from a less rational source—the racism of many anti-abolitionists themselves. Politicians, newspaper editors, and even reformers like Lyman Beecher and Horace Bushnell opposed any movement that would place the Negroes on equal terms with whites. Many anti-abolitionists simply accepted Negro inferiority as a fact and launched highly emotional, irrational attacks on the abolitionists' "desires" for a multiracial America.

In the 1830's Americans were already debating two basic political issues: the respective powers of the federal government and the states, and the possible dangers resulting from an increased electorate. Abolitionists raised the question of local versus national authority and so ran head on into an already sensitive problem. Though abolitionists did not ask for the Negro vote, they were thought to be seeking full rights for Negroes. Anti-abolitionists accused the antislavery men of being unconcerned about the political consequences of their demands, or even of intentionally fomenting discontent and problems in order to destroy the Republic. Abolitionists were also accused of using their cause as a front in order to gain power.

When anti-abolitionists argued that abolition threatened the right of states to govern their own affairs and even the continuation of the Union, they were pointing to real dangers. Abolition had been accomplished in the North on a state-by-state basis, but the new abolitionists called for national action. Furthermore, the South Carolina nullification controversy had focused attention on the possibility of disunion, and northerners were busy closing the ranks of the Union, ranks which abolition threatened to tear apart. Abolitionists challenged local authority and so threatened the

Union; they also promoted highly unpopular doctrines that might be so repugnant to southerners as to cause them to leave the Union in protest. Thus, northerners rejected antislavery not only because they feared the southern response, but also because of concern about the fate of the North, should antislavery men win their objectives. Men like James Paulding, James Austin, and the anonymous author of *A Sojourn into the City of Amalgamation* insisted that if antislavery succeeded, not only would the South secede, but those who remained in the Union would be dominated by the Negro.

The right of states to determine the fate of slavery was often linked to the argument that the slavery question was really the Negro question, and that both North and South felt this was a peculiar, inferior, race. If the Negro was inferior, what would happen to a political system in which inferior men were given equal rights? James Fenimore Cooper, Calvin Colton, Francis Wayland, and others warned about taking equality too literally. All men, they argued, were not equal in an absolute sense. If Americans came to accept Negro equality, they would believe all men were equal, and politics would simply become a contest of demagogues, each seeking to convince the people that he was going to carry equality further than his opponents. The confidence that America could absorb alien groups, weak when applied to Catholics, was almost nonexistent with regard to Negroes. The political system would be in grave danger should such groups participate in it; Negroes could easily be used by men whose sole interest was their own acquisition of power.

The problem arose as to whether men who preached subversive, potentially dangerous doctrines should be allowed to speak. Only Calvin Colton tried to focus attention on the question of whether abolition was actually seditious and so could be ended by legal means. Most of the other anti-abolitionists were not willing to consider the question at this level. Though anti-abolitionists refused, at least publicly, to condone the work of mobs, they explained mob violence as the natural outcome of the preaching of racial equality. Northerners feared that the political system would be unable to withstand such shocks.

The 1830's were a time of rapid economic change and uncertainty. To those concerned with the condition of factory workers or artisans who were hurt by competition with factory-produced goods, the abolitionist call for America to awaken to the plight of the Negro seemed to be a diversion from this major concern. More broadly, the abolitionists raised the problem of how to assure economic success for all Americans. Could the economy absorb millions of slaves once they were freed? Could the southern economy stand the loss of slave labor? Would the end of slavery mean that white men would be forced to do degrading work once done by slaves? It was entirely reasonable for labor spokesmen like Seth Luther, George Henry Evans, and the editors of the *National Trades Union* to warn of the problems of labor competition; but they became irrational when they insisted that abolitionists were agents of a wealthy class that wished to use antislavery in order to reduce wages. The fear that southerners would suffer from the loss of slave labor was also never discussed rationally. Would slaves remain on and continue to work plantation land? Was slavery more profitable than the use of free labor? Anti-abolitionists failed to ask such questions, but instead took the position that ending slavery and destroying southern economic life were synonymous. Thus the abolitionists ran afoul of northern confidence in the existing economic system, and of northern anxiety as to the future of that system. Anti-abolition took the form of emotional attack rather than reasonable debate.

The combination of confidence and anxiety, evident in northern attitudes toward political and economic development, was also apparent in a more general attitude toward the future of American society. This was an age of reform, but abolitionist insistence on complete eradication of the evil—slavery—was not consistent with contemporary reform thinking.

A common belief of the 1830's was that God had chosen America to be the place where man would succeed in establishing an ideal society. The old Puritan vision of the City on a Hill had never died. Benjamin Franklin, George Washington, and in this era Andrew Jackson epitomized the American belief that the country had combined the best of nature and civilization. But this optimism, so often expressed in an extreme chauvinism, rested partly on the feeling that anything so good must constantly be on guard lest it fall from grace. Americans of this period read their Bible and took it literally; the conflict of good and evil was very real to them. The abolitionists pointed out a basic flaw in American life. But anti-abolitionists insisted that the flaw was a carry-over from pre-Revolutionary days, an English institution; or they denied it was a flaw at all and developed defenses of slavery, calling it a humane way to treat an inferior people. Those who recognized slavery as an evil were quick to point out that the only proper way to end it was to remove the Negro from American society; accordingly, they supported colonization. In fact, most pre-Civil War reform movements did not demand the complete elimination of the evil they worked against. Thus, temperance men accepted that some men would always drink and simply called on the rest of society to insulate themselves from the evildoers. Abolitionists demanded an end to the evil and were intolerant of the slaveholder; but this was both too great an admission of an American failure and too unreasonable a demand on man and God for northerners to accept. Thus, even many of the clergy evaded the issue by denying that slavery was a moral problem or arguing that, even if it was a moral issue, abolition was not the moral way to resolve it.

In sum, the abolitionists offered the North a set of views and recommendations for action that could well be characterized as unreasonable, radical, dangerous, and unlawful.

Yet, the anti-abolitionists were not content to point out the flaws in antislavery logic, the legal and perhaps even moral grounds for rejecting the abolitionists' views and programs. Escapism as well as irrationality were evident in the anti-abolitionist arguments. This escapism and irrationalism resulted as much from exaggerated confidence and anxiety as from the real issues involved.

Between 1840 and 1860 the relation between abolitionists and the northern public underwent significant change. As late as 1860 or even 1863, the date of the New York anti-Negro "draft riots," northerners were still prejudiced against Negroes. However, that prejudice no longer was manifested in violence against abolitionists. The Texas question, the Mexican War, the struggle over slavery in Kansas, etc., all point to increasing rather than decreasing problems; yet, abolitionists now had found a place in the North as legitimate critics of an aspect of American life. Nationalism was growing stronger—as evidenced in the Know-Nothing movement, the strength of the Constitutional Union party, and the nationalist pose now assumed by both the North and South. But nationalism no longer claimed antislavery as its enemy. In 1837 John Quincy Adams stood almost alone among respectable New Englanders willing to allow abolitionists free speech. In 1856 moderate antislavery supporters like Charles Sumner represented the Bay State in Congress, and Theodore Parker and others were willing to break the law in fighting the Fugitive Slave Act. Garrison, who was mobbed in the

1830's, found a large and interested audience in the 1850's. Antislavery still had not captured the North, but it was now an acceptable reform movement, a respectable cause, since it sought to assure the secular and theological future of the country in the face of its enemies, the slaveholders.

In the 1830's anti-abolitionists rejected antislavery out of both their optimism and pessimism about the condition of America. However, in the 1850's the "slave power" became the accepted cause of tension. We are familiar with the reaction of northerners to the events of the 1850's. Southern acts of violence and accusations against the North combined to convince northerners that the South threatened the security of the nation. The abolitionists, as Russel Nye points out, encouraged that belief.[2]

The sources of public opinion we have here surveyed reflected and shaped the new abolitionist image. Politicians like William Seward, who in the 1830's had rejected the antislavery cause, in the 1850's found it convenient and politically valuable to support abolition. Reformers such as the Beechers and Charles G. Finney, who in the 1830's had rejected antislavery, now found abolition a deserving cause —while the press, which in the thirties had branded abolitionists as conspirators perpetrating acts of violence, leveled the same charges against the South. Romantic novels about the South, so popular in the North during the 1830's, were disappearing in the 1850's. Instead northerners now read Harriet Beecher Stowe's sentimental novel of family disruption and the evils of slavery and were critical of the slave system and of at least some of those who were involved in it. Thus, though they failed to change northern attitudes toward the Negro and still were unable to convince most northerners that they had the remedy to the slavery problem, the abolitionists of the 1840's and 1850's found they were no longer the enemies of the people. The southern slaveholder, rather than the abolitionist, was the target of attack; for now the slaveholder personified the threat to American confidence and provided the basis for American anxieties.

NOTES

1. This combination of confidence and anxiety has been noted or can be observed in a number of recent studies of the period. It is pointed out by Marvin Meyers, *The Jacksonian Persuasion* (Vintage ed., New York, 1957), and by William Taylor, *Cavalier and Yankee* (New York, 1961). Paul Nagle, *One Nation Indivisible* (New York, 1964), and George Dangerfield, *The Awakening of American Nationalism* (New York, 1965), provide evidence of the tension between nationalism and localism. R. W. B. Lewis, *American Adam* (Chicago, 1955), and Leo Marx, *The Machine in the Garden* (New York, 1964), study the theme as found in the literature of the time. The problem of fear of foreign conspiracy is most interestingly handled by Ray Billington, *The Protestant Crusade* (New York, 1938), and recently by David Davis, "Some Themes of Counter-Subversion." *Mississippi Valley Historical Review,* XLVII (September, 1960), 205–224. Meyers, *op. cit.,* Bray Hammond, *Banks and Politics in America from the Revolution to the Civil War* (Princeton, 1957), and Arthur Schlesinger, Jr., *The Age of Jackson* (Boston, 1953), all provide evidence of both economic disruption and success in the 1830's. The view of pre-Civil War reform as a move-

ment more concerned with isolating than with eradicating evil is presented by Timothy Smith, *Revivalism and Social Reform in Mid-Nineteenth Century America* (Nashville, 1957), by Clifford Griffin, *Their Brothers' Keepers* (New Brunswick, 1960), and others.
2. See Russel Nye, *Fettered Freedom* (East Lansing, Mich., 1949).

Bibliography

I. INTRODUCTION

I have organized the following bibliography to suggest the techniques used in preparing this volume. In each category selection has been made from a much larger body of material. Only some of the sources consulted are included in the bibliography.

To develop my topic it was necessary to become familiar with a variety of literature. I read both historical and sociological literature dealing with the Negro in the North. In order to become familiar with abolitionist activities and programs I consulted general studies of the antislavery movement, biographies of antislavery leaders, and primary source material. I also sought information as to the general tone of northern life in the 1830's.

The next step was to discover reactions to what abolitionists proposed, what people thought they proposed, and what they thought these reformers might propose. I searched newspapers, magazines, general literature, reports of religious and political organizations, and published statements of religious and political leaders. Although I had to exercise selection in my choice of materials to survey, I sought representative elements in each category. Finally I looked for specific reactions to abolition and not just evidences of anti-abolition.

II. THE NEGRO IN AMERICA BEFORE 1840

Allport, Gordon. *The Nature of Prejudice.* Abr. ed., New York, 1958.

Andrews, Charles C. *The History of the New York African Free Schools.* New York, 1830.

Anon. *An Inquiry Into the Condition and Prospects of the African Race in the United States and the Means of Bettering Its Fortunes.* Philadelphia, 1839.

Aptheker, Herbert. *A Documentary History of the Negro People in the United States.* New York, 1951.

Aptheker, Herbert. *The Negro in the Abolitionist Movement.* New York, 1941. (Pamphlet.)

Aptheker, Herbert. *Slave Insurrections in the United States, 1800–1860.* Boston, 1938.

Aptheker, Herbert. *To Be Free.* New York, 1948.

Brawley, Benjamin. *A Short History of the American Negro.* New York, 1913.

Brawley, Benjamin. *A Social History of the American Negro.* New York, 1921.

Brown, Sterling. *The Negro in American Fiction.* Washington, D.C., 1937. (Pamphlet.)

Butcher, Margaret J. *The Negro in American Culture.* New York, 1957.

Carroll, Joseph C. *Slave Insurrections in the United States, 1800–1865.* Boston, 1938.

Catterall, Helen T. *Judicial Cases Concerning American Slavery and the Negro.* 4 vols. Washington, D.C., 1936.

Dubois, William E. B. *The Philadelphia Negro, A Social Study.* Philadelphia, 1899.

Dubois, William E. B. *The Suppression of the African Slave-Trade to the United States of America, 1638–1870.* Rev. ed. New York, 1954.

Dykes, Eva B. *The Negro in English Romantic Thought.* Washington, D.C., 1942.

Freeman, F. Yardee. *A Plea for Africa.* Philadelphia, 1836.

Frazier, E. Franklin. *The Negro in the United States.* Rev. ed., New York, 1957.

Greene, Lorenzo J. *The Negro in Colonial New England.* New York, 1942.

Hartgrove, William B. "The Negro Soldier in the American Revolution," *Journal of Negro History,* I (April, 1916), 110–131.

Haynes, Leonard L., Jr. *The Negro Community within American Protestantism, 1619–1844.* Boston, 1953.

Herskovits, Melville J. *The Myth of the Negro Past.* New York, 1941.

Hirsch, Leo H. "The Negro in New York, 1783 to 1865," *Journal of Negro History,* XVI (October, 1931), 382–473.

Johnson, James W. *Black Manhattan.* New York, 1940.

Kallen, Horace M. *Cultural Pluralism and the American Idea.* Philadelphia, 1956.

Litwack, Leon. *North of Slavery.* Chicago, Ill., 1961.

Mehlinger, Louis R. "The Attitude of the Free Negro toward African Colonization," *Journal of Negro History,* I (July, 1916), 276–301.

Myrdal, Gunnar. *An American Dilemma.* New York, 1944.

Odum, Howard. *Race and Rumors of Race.* Chapel Hill, N. C., 1943.

Penn, I. Garland. *The Afro-American Press and Its Editors.*
Springfield, Mass., 1891.

Quarles, Benjamin. "The Colonial Militia and Negro Manpower,"
Mississippi Valley Historical Review, XIV (March, 1959),
643–652.

Ruchames, Louis. "Jim Crow Railroads in Massachusetts," *American Quarterly,* VIII, (Spring, 1956), 61–75.

Ruchames, Louis. "Race, Marriage, Abolition in Massachusetts,"
Journal of Negro History, XL (July, 1955), 250–273.

Samuelson, Babette. "The Patterning of Attitudes and Beliefs
Regarding the American Negro: An Analysis of Public
Opinion." Unpublished Ph.D. dissertation, Radcliffe, 1945,
Boston.

Simpson, George E. and Yinger, J. Milton. *Racial and Cultural
Minorities.* New York, 1953.

Tannenbaum, Frank. *Slave and Citizen: The Negro in the Americas.* New York, 1947.

Turner, Edward R. *The Negro in Pennsylvania, Slavery-Servitude-Freedom, 1639–1861.* Washington, D.C., 1911.

Wagley, Charles and Harris, Marvin. *Minorities in the New
World.* New York, 1958.

Warner, Robert A. *New Haven Negroes: A Social History.* New
Haven, 1940.

Weatherford, W. D. *American Churches and the Negro.* Boston,
1957.

Wesley, Charles H. *Negro Labor in the United States.* New York,
1927.

Williams, George W. *History of the Negro Race in America,
1619–1880.* 2 vols. New York, 1883.

Williams, Robin. *The Reduction of Intergroup Tensions: A Survey of Research on Problems of Ethnic, Racial, and Religious
Group Relations.* (S.S.R.C. Bulletin 57.) New York, 1947.

Wish, Harvey. "Slave Insurrections before 1860," *Journal of
Southern History,* III (July, 1937), 299–320.

Wright, Marion T. "Negro Suffrage in New Jersey, 1776–1875,"

Journal of Negro History, XXXIII (April, 1948), 168–224.

Woodson, Carter. *The History of the Negro Church.* 2nd ed. Washington, D.C., 1921.

Woodson, Carter, ed. *The Mind of the Negro as Reflected in Letters Written During the Crisis, 1800–1860.* Washington, D.C., 1926.

Woodson, Carter. *Negro Orators and Their Orations.* Washington, D.C., 1925.

Woodson, Carter. *The Education of the Negro Prior to 1861: A History of the Colored People of the United States from the Beginning of Slavery to the Civil War.* New York, 1915.

III. ATTITUDES AND VALUES IN THE 1830's

Bendix, Reinhard. *Work and Authority in Industry.* New York, 1956.

Blau, Joseph, ed. *Social Theories of Jacksonian Democracy.* New York, 1954.

Billington, Ray. *The Protestant Crusade, 1800–1860.* New York, 1938.

Burns, Edward M. *The American Idea of Mission.* New Brunswick, N. J., 1957.

Craven, Avery. *Civil War in the Making.* Baton Rouge, La., 1959.

Craven, Avery. *The Coming of the Civil War.* 2nd ed. Chicago, 1957.

Cross, Whitney. *The Burned-Over District.* Ithaca, N. Y., 1952.

Curti, Merle. *The Roots of American Loyalty.* New York, 1946.

Davis, David B. *Homicide in American Fiction, 1789–1860.* Ithaca, N. Y., 1957.

Farnam, Henry W. *Chapters in the History of Social Legislation in the United States to 1860.* Washington, D.C., 1938.

Floan, Howard R. *The South in Northern Eyes.* Austin, Texas, 1958.

Foner, Philip. *The History of the Labor Movement in the United States.* New York, 1947.

Miller, Perry. "The Romantic Dilemma in American Nationalism and the Concept of Nature," *Harvard Theological Review,* XLVI (October, 1955), 239–254.

Myers, Marvin. *The Jacksonian Persuasion.* Stanford, Calif., 1957.

Nevins, Allan. *Ordeal of the Union.* 2 vols. New York, 1947.

Osterweis, Roland. *Romanticism and Nationalism in the Old South.* New Haven, 1949.

Paul, Sherman. *The Shores of America.* Urbana, Ill., 1958.

Riegel, Robert E. *Young America.* Norman, Okla., 1949.

Rourke, Constance M. *Trumpets of Jubilee.* New York, 1927.

Schlesinger, Arthur, Jr. *The Age of Jackson.* Boston, 1953.

Smith, Timothy L. *Revivalism and Social Reform in Mid-Nineteenth-Century America.* Nashville, Tenn., 1957.

Taylor, William R. *Cavalier and Yankee.* New York, 1961.

Van Deusen, Glyndon. *The Jacksonian Era, 1828–1848.* New York, 1959.

Ward, John W. *Jackson: Symbol of an Age.* New York, 1955.

Weinberg, Albert K. *Manifest Destiny: A Study of Nationalist Expansionism in American History.* Baltimore, 1935.

IV. THE ANTISLAVERY MOVEMENTS

Abel, Annie H. and Klingburg, Frank J. *A Side-Light on Anglo-American Relations, 1839–1858.* Lancaster, Pa., 1927.

Adams, Alice D. *The Neglected Period of Anti-Slavery in America, 1808–1831.* Boston and London, 1908.

American Anti-Slavery Society Annual Reports. New York, N. Y., 1834–1840.

Barnes, Gilbert H. *The Anti-Slavery Impulse, 1830–1844.* New York and London, 1933.

Barnes, Gilbert H. and Dumond, Dwight L., eds. *Letters of Theodore Dwight Weld, Angelina Grimké Weld and Sarah Grimké.* 2 vols. New York, 1934.

Barrows, E. P. "A View of the American Slavery Question." New York, 1836.

Bassett, William. *Letter from William Bassett* (American Anti-Slavery Society Tract). Lynn, Mass., 1839.

Beecher, Catherine E. *An Essay on Slavery and Abolitionism.* Philadelphia, 1837.

Beecher, Edward. *Narrative of Riots at Alton in Connection with the Death of Rev. Elijah P. Lovejoy.* Alton, Ill., 1838.

Birney, James G. *The Letters of James Gillespie Birney.* Dumond, Dwight L., ed. 2 vols. New York, 1938.

Birney, William. *James G. Birney and His Times.* New York, 1890.

Brown, Arthur W. *Always Young for Liberty.* Syracuse, N. Y., 1956.

Channing, William E. *A Letter to the Abolitionists.* Boston, 1837.

Channing, William E. *A Letter to the Hon. Henry Clay on the Annexation of Texas to the United States.* Boston, 1837.

Channing, William E. *Slavery.* Boston, 1835.

Channing, William E. *Works.* 19th ed., 6 vols. Boston, 1869.

Child, Lydia M. *The Oasis.* Boston, 1834.

Commager, Henry S. *Theodore Parker.* Boston, 1936.

Curti, Merle. "Reformers Consider the Constitution," *American Journal of Sociology,* XLIII (May, 1938), 878–893.

Dillon, Merton, "The Failure of the Abolitionists," *Journal of Southern History,* XXV (May, 1959), 159–177.

Donald, David. *Lincoln Reconsidered: Essays on the Civil War Era.* New York, 1956.

Dumond, Dwight L. *Anti-Slavery Origins of the Civil War.* Ann Arbor, Michigan, 1959.

Dumond, Dwight L. "Race Prejudice and Abolition," *Michigan Alumnus Quarterly Review,* XLI (April, 1935), 377–385.

Bibliography

Dyson, Zita. "Gerritt Smith and the Negro," *Journal of Negro History,* III (October, 1918), 354–359.

Earle, Thomas. *The Life, Travels, and Opinions of Benjamin Lundy.* Philadelphia, 1847.

Edgell, David P. *William Ellery Channing: An Intellectual Portrait.* Boston, 1955.

Elkins, Stanley M. *Slavery: A Problem in American Institutional and Intellectual Life.* Chicago, 1959.

Fladeland, Betty. *James Birney; Slaveholder and Abolitionist.* Ithaca, N. Y., 1955.

Foner, Philip. *Business and Slavery: The New York Merchants and the Irrepressible Conflict.* Chapel Hill, N. C., 1941.

Fox, Early L. *The American Colonization Society, 1817–1840.* Baltimore, 1919.

Garrison, F. P. and Garrison, W. P. *William Lloyd Garrison, 1805–1879.* 4 vols. New York, 1885–1889.

Garrison, William L. *Selections from the Speeches and Writings of William Lloyd Garrison.* Boston, 1852.

Garrison, William L. *Thoughts on African Colonization.* Boston, 1832.

Goodell, William. *Slavery and Anti-Slavery, History of the Great Struggle in both Hemispheres; with a View to the Slavery Question in the United States.* New York, 1852.

Gill, John. *Tide Without Turning: Elijah P. Lovejoy and Freedom of the Press.* Boston, 1958.

Harlow, Ralph V. *Gerrit Smith, Philanthropist and Reformer.* New York, 1939.

Hart, Albert B. *Slavery and Abolition.* New York, 1906.

Jenkins, William S. *Pro-Slavery Thought in the South.* Chapel Hill, N. C., 1935.

Johnson, Oliver. *William Lloyd Garrison.* Boston and New York, 1880.

Korngold, Ralph. *Two Friends of Man: William Lloyd Garrison and Wendell Phillips.* Boston, 1950.

Levy, Leonard W. "The Abolition Riot: Boston's First Slave

Rescue," *New England Quarterly,* XXV (March, 1952), 85–92.

Lloyd, Arthur Y. *The Slavery Controversy 1831–1860.* Chapel Hill, N. C., 1939.

Lowell, James Russell. *Anti-Slavery Papers.* W. B. Parker, ed. 2 vols. New York, 1902.

Lyman, Theodore. *Papers Relating to the Garrison Mob.* Cambridge, 1870.

May, Samuel. *Recollections of the Anti-Slavery Conflict.* Cambridge, Mass., 1869.

Mellon, Mathew T. *Early American Views on Negro Slavery.* Boston, 1934.

Moore, George H. *Notes on the History of Slavery in Massachusetts.* New York, 1866.

Needles, Edward. *An Historical Memoir of the Pennsylvania Society for Promoting the Abolition of Slavery.* Philadelphia, 1848.

Nye, Russel. *Fettered Freedom.* East Lansing, Michigan, 1949.

Nye, Russel. "The Slave Power Conspiracy 1830–1860," *Science and Society,* X (Summer, 1946), 262–274.

Nye, Russel. *William Lloyd Garrison and the Humanitarian Reformers.* Boston, 1955.

Parker, Theodore. *Sermons on Slavery.* Boston, 1848–1858.

Phillips, Wendell. *Speeches, Letters and Lectures.* Boston, 1863.

Power, Richard L. "A Crusade to Extend Yankee Culture," *New England Quarterly,* XIII (December, 1940), 638–653.

Rush, Benjamin. *An Address to the Inhabitants of the British Colonies in America Upon Slavekeeping.* Norwich, England, 1775.

Sewall, Samuel E. *Remarks on Slavery in the United States.* Boston, 1827.

Sherwin, Oscar. *Prophet of Liberty: The Life and Times of Wendell Phillips.* New York, 1958.

Siebert, William H. *The Underground Railroad: from Slavery to Freedom.* New York, 1898.

Bibliography

Skotheim, Robert. "A Note on Historical Method: David Donald's 'Toward a Reconsideration of Abolitionists,'" *Journal of Southern History,* XXV (August, 1959), 356–365.

Small, E. W. and Small, M. R. "Prudence Crandall," *New England Quarterly,* XVII (December, 1944), 506–529.

Stampp, Kenneth. "The Fate of Southern Anti-Slavery," *Journal of Negro History,* XXVIII (January, 1943), 10–22.

Stanton, Henry B. *Remarks in the Representatives Hall on the 23rd and 24th of February, before the Committee of the House of Representatives of Massachusetts. . . .* Boston, 1837.

Stanton, Henry B. *Random Recollections.* New York, 1887.

Swift, Lindsay. *William Lloyd Garrison.* Philadelphia, 1911.

Tappan, Arthur. "Correspondence," *Journal of Negro History,* XII (April, 1927), 179–329.

Tappan, Lewis. *Arthur Tappan.* New York, 1870.

Thistlethwaite, Frank. *The Anglo-American Connection in the Early Nineteenth Century.* Philadelphia, 1959.

Thomas, Benjamin P. *Theodore Weld.* New Brunswick, N. J., 1950.

Weld, Theodore. *Bible against Slavery.* New York, 1838.

Whitfield, Theodore M. *Slavery Agitation in Virginia, 1829–1832.* Baltimore, 1930.

Wolf, Hazel C. *On Freedom's Altar: The Martyr Complex in the Abolition Movement.* Madison, Wisconsin, 1952.

V. NEWSPAPERS AND MAGAZINES

Advocate (changed in 1838 to the *Colored American.* New York and Philadelphia), 1837–1839.

African Repository (Washington, D.C.), 1831–1840.

Albany Argus, 1835–1837.

American Quarterly Observer (Boston), 1831–1840.

American Quarterly Review (Philadelphia), 1831–1840.

Atkinson's Saturday Evening Post (Philadelphia), 1833–1839.
Baptist Magazine (London, England), 1833–1839.
Bay State Democrat (Boston), 1838–1839.
Bentley's Miscellany (London, England), 1831–1840.
Biblical Repertory and Theological Review (Philadelphia), 1831–1840.
Blackwood's Magazine (London, England), 1832–1840.
Boston Atlas, 1838–1839.
Boston Quarterly Review, 1838–1839.
Boston Recorder, 1831–1840.
Boston Transcript, 1831–1840.
Chamberlin, Joseph E. *The Boston Transcript.* Cambridge, Mass., 1930.
Christian Advocate (Philadelphia), 1834.
Christian Examiner and General Review (Boston), 1831–1839.
Christian Intelligencer (New York), 1832–1838.
Eastern Argus (Portland, Me.), 1835–1837.
Edinburgh Review (Edinburgh, Scotland), 1831–1840.
Emancipator (New York), 1835.
Emporium and True American (Trenton, N. J.), 1837–1839.
Godey's Ladies Book (Philadelphia), 1831–1839.
Ithaca Chronicle (Ithaca, N. Y.), 1835–1839.
Ithaca Journal (Ithaca, N. Y.), 1836–1839.
Jesuit or Catholic Sentinel (changed to *The Pilot*) (Boston), 1831–1838.
Kennebec Weekly Journal (Augusta, Me.), 1831–1838.
Knickerbocker Magazine (New York), 1835–1840.
Liberator (Boston), 1831–1840.
Massachusetts Abolitionist (Boston), 1839.
Mechanics Magazine (New York), 1833–1837.
National Trades Union (New York), 1834–1837.
Nevins, Allan. *American Press Opinion: Washington to Coolidge.* New York, 1928.
New Bedford Daily Gazette (New Bedford, Mass.), 1833–1835.
New Bedford Mercury (New Bedford, Mass.), 1833–1839.

Bibliography

Newburyport Daily Herald (Newburyport, Mass.), 1832–1839.
New England Farmer and Horticultural Journal (Boston), 1833–
1839.
New England Magazine (Boston), 1832–1839.
New Jersey Journal (Elizabethtown, N. J.), 1835–1839.
New York Commercial Advertiser, 1832–1837.
New York Evangelist, 1835–1837.
New York Evening Post, 1831–1837.
New York Herald, 1835–1839.
New York Journal of Commerce, 1831–1839.
New York Review and Quarterly Church Journal, 1837–1839.
Niles's Register (Baltimore), 1820–1840.
North American Review (Boston), 1831–1839.
Norwich Courier (Norwich, Conn.), 1831–1837.
Pennsylvanian (Philadelphia), 1831–1839.
Princeton Whig, 1835–1839.
Quarterly Christian Spectator (New Haven), 1832–1837.
Quarterly Register of the American Educational Society (Boston),
1831–1835.
Reformed Presbyterian (Newburgh, N. Y.), 1838–1839.
Religious Monitor and Evangelical Repository (Albany, N. Y.),
1831–1839.
Rhode Island Country Journal (Providence), 1833–1837.
United States Gazette (Philadelphia), 1831–1839.
United States Magazine and Democratic Review (New York),
1838–1840.
Zion's Watchman (New York), 1836.

VI. NOVELS, PLAYS, TRAVEL BOOKS, AND
SOCIAL COMMENTARY

Anon. *The Reign of Reform or Yankee Doodle Court.* Baltimore, 1830.

Beaumont, Gustave de. *Marie, or Slavery in the United States.* New ed. Stanford, Calif., 1959.

Bickley, Lloyd. *The Aristocrat: An American Tale.* 2 vols. Philadelphia, 1833.

Bird, Robert M. *The City Looking Glass: A Philadelphia Comedy.* New York, 1933.

Bird, Robert M. *Nick of the Woods.* Rev. ed. New York, 1939.

Bird, Robert M. *Peter Pilgrim.* 2 vols. Philadelphia, 1838.

Bird, Robert M. *Sheppard Lee.* 2 vols. New York, 1836.

Bolokitten, Oliver (pseud.) *A Sojourn in the City of Amalgamation in the Year of Our Lord 19——.* New York, 1835.

Brothers, Thomas. *The United States of North America As They Are; Not As They Are Generally Described: Being a Cure for Radicalism.* London, England, 1840.

Carruthers, William A. *The Cavaliers of Virginia; or the Recluse of Jamestown.* 2 vols. New York, 1834–1835.

Carruthers, William A. *The Kentuckian in New York or the Adventures of Three Southerners.* 2 vols. New York, 1834.

Cooper, James F. *The American Democrat.* New ed. New York, 1931.

Cooper, James F. *Correspondence of James Fenimore Cooper,* James F. Cooper, ed. 4 vols. New Haven, Conn., 1922.

Cooper, James F. *Home as Found.* Leatherstocking ed. New York, 1896.

Cooper, James F. *Homeward Bound.* Leatherstocking ed. New York, 1896.

Cooper, James F. *The Last of the Mohicans.* Leatherstocking ed. New York, 1896.

Emerson, Ralph W. *Journals.* Edward W. Emerson and Waldo C. Forbes, eds. 10 vols. Boston, 1909.

Foust, Clement E. *Robert Montgomery Bird: Life and Dramatic Works.* New York, 1919.

Gilman, Caroline. *Recollections of a New England Bride and a Southern Matron.* New York, 1838.

Greene, Asa. *Travels in America.* New York, 1833.

Grossman, James. *James Fenimore Cooper.* New York, 1949.

Hall, Captain Basil. *Travels in North America in the Years 1827–1828.* 2nd ed. 3 vols. Edinburgh, 1830.

Herold, Amos L. *James Kirke Paulding: Versatile American.* New York, 1926.

Kennedy, John P. *Swallow Barn or a Sojourn in the Old Dominion.* Philadelphia, 1832.

McClung, John A. *Camden, A Tale of the South.* 2 vols. Philadelphia, 1830.

Martineau, Harriet. *Society in America.* 2 vols. New York, 1837.

Martineau, Harriet. *Retrospect of Western Travel.* 3 vols. London, England, 1838.

Mesick, Jane L. *The English Traveler in America 1785–1835.* New York, 1922.

Murray, Charles A. *Travels in North America.* 2 vols. New York, 1839.

Paulding, James K. *Letters from the South by a Northern Man.* New York, 1835.

Paulding, James K. *The Lion of the West.* New ed. Stanford, California, 1954.

Paulding, James K. *Slavery in the United States.* New York, 1836.

Pierson, George W. *Beaumont and Tocqueville in America.* New York, 1938.

Quinn, A. H. *A History of the American Drama.* Rev. ed. New York, 1943.

Spiller, Robert E.; Thorpe, Willard; Johnson, Thomas; Canby, Henry S., eds. *Literary History of the United States.* Rev. ed. New York, 1955.

Tocqueville, Alexis de. *Democracy in America.* New ed. 2 vols.
New York, 1945.
Trollope, Frances. *Domestic Manners of the Americans.* 4th ed.
London and New York, 1832.
Turner, Lorenzo D. "Anti-Slavery Sentiment in American Litera-
ture," *Journal of Negro History, XIV* (October, 1929),
371–492.
A Virginian (pseud.). *Rose-Hill.* Philadelphia, 1835.

VII. THE CHURCHES AND ABOLITION

Andrews, Rena M. "Slavery Views of a Northern Prelate," *Church
History,* III (March, 1934), 60–78.
Armstrong, Maurice W., Loetscher, Lefferts A., Anderson, Charles
A., eds. *The Presbyterian Enterprise, Sources of American
Presbyterian History.* Philadelphia, 1956.
Bacon, Theodore D. *Leonard Bacon.* New Haven, 1931.
Barclay, Crawford. *Early American Methodism.* 2 vols. New York,
1949.
Barnes, Albert, *The Church and Slavery.* Philadelphia, 1857.
Beecher, Lyman. *Autobiography and Correspondence of Lyman
Beecher.* Charles Beecher, ed. 2 vols. New York, 1865.
Bodo, John R. *The Protestant Clergy and Public Issues, 1812–
1848.* Princeton, N. J., 1954.
Brokhage, Rev. Joseph D. *Francis Patrick Kenricks' Opinion on
Slavery.* Washington, D.C., 1955.
Brookes, George S. *Friend Anthony Benezet.* Philadelphia, 1937.
Bushnell, Horace. *A Discourse on the Slavery Question. Delivered
in the North Church, Hartford, Connecticut, January 10,
1839.*
Clark, Calvin M. *American Slavery and Maine Congregationalists.*
Bangor, Maine, 1940.
Cole, Charles C., Jr. "Horace Bushnell and the Slavery Question,"
New England Quarterly, XXIII (March, 1950), 19–30.

Bibliography

Cole, Charles C. *The Social Ideas of Northern Evangelists.* New York, 1954.

Colton, Calvin. *The Genius and Mission of the Protestant Episcopal Church in the United States.* New York, 1853.

Cooke, George Willis. *Unitarianism in America.* Boston, 1902.

Cox, Rev. F. A. and Hoby, Rev. J. *The Baptists in America.* New York, 1836.

Debate on Modern Abolitionism in the General Conference of the Methodist Episcopal Church. Cincinnati, 1836.

Discussion on American Slavery between George Thompson and Rev. Robert J. Breckenridge. Boston, 1836.

Drake, Thomas E. *Quakers and Slavery in America.* New Haven, 1950.

Drury, Clifford M. *Presbyterian Panorama.* Philadelphia, 1952.

Fortenbaugh, Robert. "American Lutheran Synods and Slavery, 1830–1860," *Journal of Religion,* XIII (January, 1933), 72–92.

Foss, A. T. and Mathews, E. *Facts for Baptist Churches.* Utica, N. Y., 1850.

Griffin, Clifford S. "The Abolitionists and the Benevolent Societies, 1831–1861," *Journal of Negro History,* XLIV (July, 1959), 195–216.

Griffin, Clifford S. "Religious Benevolence as Social Control, 1815–1860," *Mississippi Valley Historical Review,* XLIV (December, 1957), 423–444.

Kreider, Harry J. *History of the United Lutheran Synod of New York and New England.* 2 vols. Philadelphia, 1954.

Kull, Irving. "Presbyterian Attitudes Toward Slavery," *Church History,* VII (June, 1938), 101–114.

Lyons, Adelaide A. *Religious Defense of Slavery in the North.* (Historical Papers Published by the Trinity College Historical Society, Series XIII.) Durham, N. C., 1919.

McLouglin, William G. *Modern Revivalism.* New York, 1959.

McMaster, Gilbert. *The Moral Character of Civil Government*

Considered with Reference to the Political Institutions of the United States. Duanesburgh, N. Y., 1832.

Manross, William W. *The Episcopal Church in the United States, 1800–1840.* New York, 1938.

Moore, Edmund A. "Robert J. Breckenridge and the Slavery Aspect of the Presbyterian Schism of 1837," *Church History,* IV (December, 1935), 282–294.

Norwood, John N. *The Schism in the Methodist Episcopal Church, 1844.* Alfred, N. Y., 1923.

Nueremberger, Ruth A. *The Free Produce Movement: A Quaker Protest against Slavery.* Durham, N. C., 1942.

Pennington, Edgar L. "Thomas Bray's Associates and Their Work among the Negroes," *Proceedings of the American Antiquarian Society* (October, 1938), pp. 311–403.

Rice, Madeline H. *American Catholic Opinion in the Slavery Controversy.* New York, 1944.

Shea, Joseph M. "The Baptists and Slavery, 1840–1845." (Unpublished M.A. dissertation. Clark University, 1933.)

Staiger, C. Bruce. "Abolitionism and the Presbyterian Schism of 1837–1838," *Mississippi Valley Historical Review,* XXXVI (December, 1949), 391–414.

Swaney, Charles B. *Episcopal Methodism and Slavery.* Boston, 1926.

Wayland, Francis. *The Limitations of Human Responsibility.* Boston, 1838.

Weisburger, Bernard A. *They Gathered at the River.* Boston, 1958.

Whedon, Daniel D. *Essays, Reviews and Discourses.* J. S. Whedon and D. A. Whedon, eds. New York, 1887.

Whipple, Charles K. *Relation of the American Board of Commissioners for Foreign Missions to Slavery.* Boston, 1861.

Woodson, Carter, "Anthony Benezet," *Journal of Negro History,* II (January, 1917). 37–50.

Woolman, John. *Extracts on the Subject of Slavery from the Journal and Writings of John Woolman.* New York, 1840.

Bibliography

VIII. NORTHERN POLITICIANS AND ABOLITION

Adams, John. *Works.* Charles F. Adams, ed. 10 vols. Boston, 1856.
Adams, John Quincy. *The Diary of John Quincy Adams, 1794–1845.* Allan Nevins, ed. New York, 1928.
Austin, James T. *Remarks on Dr. Channing's Slavery by a Citizen of Massachusetts.* Boston, 1835.
Bancroft, Frederick. *Life of William H. Seward.* 2 vols. New York, 1900.
Bemis, Samuel F. *John Quincy Adams and the Union.* New York, 1956.
Brodie, Fawn. *Thaddeus Stevens.* New York, 1959.
Burden, J. R. *Remarks of J. R. Burden of Philadelphia County in the Senate of Pennsylvania on the Abolition Question.* Philadelphia, 1838.
Byrdsall, F. *The History of the Loco-Foco or Equal Rights Party.* New York, 1842.
Coles, Edward. "Letters of Gov. Coles of Illinois." *Journal of Negro History,* II (April, 1918).
Colton, Calvin. *Abolition a Sedition.* Philadelphia, 1839.
Colton, Calvin. *The Americans.* London, England, 1833.
Colton, Calvin. *Colonization and Abolition Contrasted.* Philadelphia, 1839.
Current, Richard N. *Old Thad Stevens.* Madison, Wisc., 1942.
Darling, Arthur B. *Political Changes in Massachusetts.* New Haven, 1925.
Detweiler, Phillip F. "Congressional Debate on Slavery and the Declaration of Independence, 1819–1821," *American Historical Review,* LXIII (April, 1958), 598–616.
Frothingham, Paul R. *Edward Everett.* Boston and New York, 1925.
Fuess, Claude M. *The Life of Caleb Cushing.* 2 vols. New York, 1923.

Fuess, Claude M. "Daniel Webster and the Abolitionists," *Massachusetts Historical Society Proceedings,* LXIV (November, 1930), 28–49.

Greeley, Horace. *Recollections of a Busy Life.* New York, 1868.

Howe, Mark D. W. *The Life and Letters of George Bancroft.* 2 vols. New York, 1908.

Moore, Glover. *The Missouri Controversy, 1819–1821.* Lexington, Ky., 1953.

Morison, Samuel Eliot. *The Life and Letters of Harrison Gray Otis, Federalist, 1765–1848.* 2 vols. Boston, 1913.

Parton, James. *Famous Americans of Recent Times.* Boston, 1867.

Rantoul, Robert, Jr. *Memoirs, Speeches and Writings of Robert Rantoul, Jr.* Luther Hamilton, ed. Boston, 1854.

Report of the Committee Appointed to Draft Resolutions Relative to the Proceedings of the Advocates of Immediate Abolition of Slavery in the Southern States. Presented to the New Hampshire House of Representatives, January 11, 1837.

Sellers, Charles G. *James Polk, Jacksonian, 1795–1843.* Princeton, N. J., 1957.

Snyder, Charles M. *The Jacksonian Heritage: Pennsylvania Politics 1833–1848.* Harrisburg, 1958.

Stearns, Frank P. *The Life and Public Services of George Luther Stearns.* Philadelphia, 1907.

Story, William W. *The Life and Letters of Joseph Story.* 2 vols. Boston, 1851.

Tiffany, Nina M. *Samuel E. Sewall, A Memoir.* Boston and New York, 1898.

Trimble, William. "New York Democracy and the Locofocos," *American Historical Review,* XXIV (April, 1919), 396–421.

Tuckerman, Bayard. *William Jay and the Constitutional Movement for the Abolition of Slavery.* New York, 1893.

Van Deusen, Glyndon. *Horace Greeley.* Philadelphia, 1953.

Webster, Daniel. *Speeches and Writings.* J. W. McIntyre, ed. 18 vols. Boston, 1903.

Bibliography

Zahler, Helene S. *Eastern Workingmen and National Land Policy, 1829–1862.* New York, 1941.

IX. OTHER REACTIONS TO ABOLITION

Brown, Sterling. "Negro Character as Seen by White Authors," *Journal of Negro Education,* II (April, 1933), 179–203.

Commons, John R., *et al.,* eds. *Documentary History of American Industrial Society.* 10 vols. Cleveland, Ohio, 1910–1911.

Commons, John R., *et al. History of Labour in the United States.* 4 vols. New York, 1918–1935.

Ernst, Robert. *Immigrant Life in New York City, 1825–1863,* New York, 1949.

Gibson, Florence E. *The Attitudes of the New York Irish toward State and National Affairs.* New York, 1951.

Hartz, Lewis. "Seth Luther, Working-Class Rebel," *New England Quarterly,* XIII (September, 1940), 401–418.

Jefferson, Thomas. "Thomas Jefferson's Thoughts on the Negro." *Journal of Negro History,* III (Jan. 1918). Edited writings.

Jefferson, Thomas. *The Works of Thomas Jefferson.* Paul L. Ford, ed. 12 vols. New York, 1904–1905.

Madison, James. "James Madison's Attitudes toward the Negro." *Journal of Negro History,* VI (Jan. 1921), 74–112. Edited writings.

Madison, James. *The Writings of James Madison.* Gaillard Hunt, ed. 9 vols. New York, 1900.

Lofton, William H. "Abolition and Labor," *Journal of Negro History,* XXXIII (July, 1948), 249–283.

Mandel, Bernard. *Labor, Free and Slave.* New York, 1955.

Morse, Samuel F. B. *Foreign Conspiracy against the Liberties of the United States.* 6th ed. New York, 1844.

Morse, Samuel F. B. *Samuel F. B. Morse, Letters and Journals.* Edward L. Morse, ed. 2 vols. Boston, 1914.

Rayback, Joseph. "The American Workingman and the Anti-

Slavery Crusade," *Journal of Economic History,* III (November, 1943), 152–163.

Reese, Dr. David M. *A Brief Review of the First Annual Report of the American Anti-Slavery Society.* . . . New York, 1834.

Reese, Dr. David M. *Humbugs of New York.* New York, 1838.

Smith, Samuel S. *An Essay on the Causes of the Variety of Complexion and Figure in the Human Species.* 2nd ed. New Brunswick, N. J., 1810.

Stanton, William L. *The Leopard's Spots: Scientific Attitudes toward Race in America, 1815–1859.* Chicago, 1960.

Washington, George. *The Writings of George Washington.* John C. Fitzpatrick, ed. 39 vols. Washington, D.C., 1931.

Wittke, Carl. *Tambo and Bones.* Durham, N. C., 1930.

Index

abolition and abolitionism: as anarchy, 73; Constitution and, 64; equality and, 58–62, 104; fear of, 23; as "primary menace," 85; racism and, 4–5; Union endangered by, 51, 56, 131

Abolition a Sedition (Colton), 55, 115

abolitionists: Churches and, 88–90; seen as impractical, 69; prejudice of, 45

Adams, John, 14, 16–18

Adams, John Quincy, 35, 80–82, 139

Address to the Workingmen of New England (Luther), 63

African Repository, 45, 60

America: multiracial dream of, 134; yeoman-artisan concept for, 62–63

American Anti-Slavery Society, 3, 94, 114

American Baptist Convention, 110–111

American Biblical Repository, 96

American Colonization Society, 16, 34, 44–45, 60, 73, 78, 98, 102, 105–106, 111, 118, 122

American Democrat, The (Cooper), 45

American manners and culture, 30–31

American Missionary Board, 90

American Quarterly Observer, 60, 69

American Revolution, 11, 111

Americans, The (Colton), 33

American Union, 99–100

Andover Theological Seminary, 40

anti-abolitionism: arguments for, 59–61; fears underlying, 70; foundations of, 131–132; intensity of, 131–132; in newspapers,

Index

anti-abolitionism (*cont'd*)
44; racism and, 5; riots and, 76,
83–84, 102; rise of, 23, 36–42
anti-Catholic feeling, 36–37, 71,
132, 135
antiforeign crusade, 36–41
anti-Masonism, 37
anti-Mormonism, 37
antislavery: Churches and, 89–90,
96, 99–124; English, 28–29;
"moderates" on, 54–55; and
Presbyterians, 96; rejection of,
23
Anti-Slavery Convention, 72
Anti-Slavery Society, 56; *see also*
American Anti-Slavery Society
anxiety, age of, 132
Austin, James T., 4, 54, 60, 79, 135

Bacon, Leonard, 105
Baltimore Friends Anti-Slavery So-
ciety, 123
Bancroft, George, 54–55
Baptist Church, antislavery and,
109–110, 113–114
Baptist Triennial Convention, 112
Barnes, Albert, 91
Barrows, E. P., 96
Bassett, William, 123
Bavarian Illuminati, 37
Beaumont, Gustave de, 29, 32–33
Beecher, Catherine, 35, 38, 46,
100–101
Beecher, Lyman, 35, 98–100, 102,
105, 133
Beecher, William, 99
Benezet, Anthony, 122

Bennett, James Gordon, 37–38, 71,
78, 83–84
Bible, slavery references in, 60, 93,
138
*Biblical Repertory and Theological
Review* (Hodge), 92–93
Bird, Robert Montgomery, 60–62,
79
Birney, James G., 64, 107
Boston, race riots in, 40–41
Boston Atlas, 81, 83
Boston Quarterly Review, 64
Boston Recorder, 101–102
Boston Transcript, 35, 38, 40–41,
45, 53–54, 60, 76, 81–82
British West Indies, race riots in,
70, 75
Brothers, Thomas, 29
Brownson, Orestes, 64
Brown University, 113
Bryant, William Cullen, 44, 84
Buchanan, James, 81
Buffum, Arnold, 123
Burden, James, 55, 73–74
Bushnell, Horace, 102–105, 133

Calhoun, John C., 52
Camden, A Tale of the South
(McClung), 43
Catholic Church, on slavery issue,
120
Catholics, feared by Protestants,
36–37, 71, 132, 135
Channing, William Ellery, 118–
120, 133
Child, Lydia Maria, 73
Christian Advocate, 97

Index

France, romantic school in, 32
Franklin, Benjamin, 11, 61, 137
Free Produce Movement, 122–123
French Revolution, 75
Friends of Humanity, 110
Fugitive Slave Act, 139

Garrison, William Lloyd, 32, 35, 39, 72, 76, 80, 82, 99, 102, 105, 118, 122–123, 139
"Garrison riot" of 1833, 35, 76
gentleman planter, image of, 42
Green, Ashabel, 97
Green, Beriah, 93–94
Greene, Asa, 31, 33
Grimké, Angelina, 100
Gurley, Ralph, 98

Hall, Basil, 29, 33
Hartford Observer, 69
Hedding, Bishop Elijah, 106, 108–109
Hicksite Quakers, 122
Hobart, Bishop John Henry, 115
Hoby, J., 112
Hodge, Charles, 91–93
Home Missionary Society, 91

Indians, Negro compared with, 16, 110
individual, and states' rights, 51–64
Irving, Washington, 18

Jackson, Andrew, 52, 98, 137
Jay, John, 61
Jefferson, Thomas, 11–14, 61
"Jim Crow" figure, 22

Kendrick, Bishop, 120
Kennebec Weekly Journal, 75
Kennedy, John Pendleton, 42
Knickerbocker Magazine, 44–45, 78

Lafayette, Marie Joseph, Marquis de, 12
Lane Theological Seminary, 93, 99
Last of the Mohicans, The (Cooper), 21
Lay, Benjamin, 10, 121
Leavitt, Joshua, 96
Lee, Luther, 109
Leggett, William, 63–64, 84
Letters from the South (Paulding), 38, 42
Letters to Presbyterians on the Present Crisis in the Presbyterian Church (Hodge), 91
Liberator, The, 40, 53, 122
Liberia, Negro colony in, 106
Limitations of Human Responsibility, The (Wayland), 113, 116
Lion of the West, The (Paulding), 23, 31
Litwack, Leon, 6
Locofocos, radical group, 38, 70
Lovejoy, Elijah, murder of, 77, 82–84, 118
Lundy, Benjamin, 122
Luther, Seth, 63, 136
Lutheran Church, antislavery and, 117

McClung, John A., 43
McMaster, Gilbert, 96
Madison, James, 11, 14–16, 18

Index

Old-School Presbyterians, 93
Otis, Harrison Gray, 82
outsiders, meddling by, 28–46

Parker, Theodore, 139
Paulding, James Kirk, 19–20, 23, 31, 38, 42, 52, 57, 59–60, 64, 73, 75, 79, 135
Pennsylvania Abolition Society, 121
Pennsylvania Hall, burning of, 77, 83, 124
Pennsylvanian, The, 20, 77–78
Pennsylvania State Constitutional Convention, 21
Peter Grimm (Bird), 61
Phelps, A. A., 114
Philadelphia: burning of Pennsylvania Hall, 77, 83, 124; Quakers in, 121–124; riots in, 20
Porter, Noah, 79
Portsmouth Weekly Journal, 77
prejudice, role of, 45
Presbyterian Church: abolitionism and, 96–97; Old-School and New-School attitudes in, 90–92
Presbyterian General Assembly, 92
Princeton Theological Seminary, 92
Protestants, fear of Catholics by, 36–37, 71, 132, 135
"Pseudo-philanthropists," 79

Quakers: antislavery stand of, 120–121; Hicksite group, 122; in Pennsylvania, 10; in Philadelphia, 121–124; in Virginia, 13

Quakers and Slavery in America (Drake), 123

race hatred, Martineau on, 116
race riots: abolitionism and, 71–72, 78–79; in Boston, 40–41; inciting of, 41; in New York City, 35; in Philadelphia, 20
race war, fear of, 77
racism: persistence of, 3–23; prejudice and, 9–10, 131–132
radicalism, fears of, 68–85
Rantoul, Robert, Jr., 54
Reese, David M., 61, 79
reform movements, 138
reform societies, 98
religion, slavery and, 137–138; *see also* Bible; churches; Presbyterian Church, *etc.*
Rhode Island Country Journal, 41
Rice, T. D. ("Jim Crow"), 22–23
riots, anti-abolitionist, 76, 83–84; *see also* draft riots; race riots
romantic novels, 140–141
Rose-Hill (anon:), 43

Saffin, John, 10
Sandiford, Ralph, 10, 121
Scott, Orange, 108
Sewall, Samuel, 10
Seward, William, 140
sexual relations, between races, 19, 78
Sheppard Lee (Bird), 60
slavery: attacks on, 10; Bible references to, 60, 93, 138; foreign criticism of, 36–39; as moral issue, 138; Northern attitude to-

Index